KU-130-099

Published by Ames Division, Miles Limited,
Stoke Court, Stoke Poges,
Buckinghamshire, SL2 4LY

© 1990 Ames Division, Miles Limited

ISBN 0 9505887 1 7 Clinical Urinalysis Pbk

# Clinical Urinalysis

Editor: **R. G. Newall**
with R. Howell

The Principles and Practice
of Urine Testing in the Hospital
and Community

Published by Ames Division, Miles Limited.

# Contents

# Contents (continued)

# Urine Analysis:
# Introduction and Overview

## Professor Vincent Marks
## Department of Biochemistry, University of Surrey, Guildford

Clinical biochemistry can be said to have had its origins in urinalysis with the introduction, by Bright, of urine testing for protein as a test for kidney damage and the differential diagnosis of oedema. With the later use of urine testing for confirmation of a clinical diagnosis of diabetes mellitus, the stage was set for the extension of chemical testing into all branches of medicine, not only those concerned with renal disease. It was, however, not until almost a hundred years had passed that urine gave way to blood as the most commonly tested body fluid for the detection and diagnosis of disease. In some large hospitals in other parts of the world there are still departments, separated physically and organisationally from the rest of the laboratory, that are used exclusively for urinalysis.

Urinalysis received an enormous fillip in recent times when dry reagents, first in the form of tablets and then in the shape of paper-impregnated strips, were introduced by the Ames Division of Miles Inc. of America. This not only took urinalysis out of the laboratory, where it had come to rest after commencing its existence at the bedside, but made it available for use by patients themselves. Originally confined to the monitoring of diabetes therapy, patient self-testing has extended into pregnancy diagnosis and, even more recently, into ovulation prediction.

*Changes in the composition of urine are sometimes the first and only indication of real or impending renal disease*

Apart from its simplicity, due both to the ease with which the specimen can be collected and the availability of suitable testing materials, urinalysis can provide information not available in any other way and certainly not as quickly. Not only are changes in the composition of urine sometimes the first and only indication of real or impending renal disease, but urinalysis may be the only practicable means of making the diagnosis of a metabolic disorder or of drug overdose and abuse. This is due not only to the great concentrating power of the kidneys, but also to their selectivity.

*Urinalysis may be the only practicable means of making the diagnosis of a metabolic disorder or of drug overdose and abuse*

*The differentiation of the cause of hyperbilirubinuria can be carried out by a urinalysis strip as simply, more quickly and equally reliably, as by standard laboratory techniques*

The differentiation of hyperbilirubinaemia caused by accumulation of unconjugated bilirubin, from that caused by hepatocellular damage can, by using a urinalysis strip, be made as simply, more quickly and equally reliably, at the bedside or in the general practitioner's office as in a laboratory employing standard analytical techniques, for example. Only very rarely is it necessary, except for research purposes, to carry out fractionation of plasma bilirubin in order to establish the type of jaundice present, providing that a urine specimen is also available for examination; all too often it is not. Rarely, in these circumstances, has the appropriate test been carried out on the ward – generally because its value was not appreciated by the junior medical staff or others responsible for performing and interpreting the results of urinalysis – as a consequence the laboratory is asked, and indeed expected, to carry out a wholly needless and unreliable investigation involving plasma bilirubin fractionation.

*Urine strip testing for bilirubin may obviate the need for plasma bilirubin fractionation by the laboratory*

It is in order to delineate and overcome some of these problems, as well as to put the value of urinalysis into perspective – including its clinical usefulness in population screening – that this book has been written. The format has been designed so as to ensure that not only disease-related uses of urinalysis are considered, but also that situations which arise as a result of the way clinical practice is ordinarily conducted are taken into account.

*Routine urinalysis is worthwhile!*

In answer to the perennial question – "Is routine urinalysis worth while?" – the answer is a resounding "YES"[1,2]. It has a very useful role to play in screening for and monitoring of a number of different conditions.

It is however, a moot point, and one that cannot readily be resolved without consideration of factors other than the purely clinical, as to how extensive routine urinalysis should be. In other words: how many analytes should be looked for and how often should tests be repeated.

With modern analytical technology, up to ten different tests can be carried out on one sample of urine as rapidly, simply and almost as cheaply as just one or two. Problems encountered in matching by eye the large number of different colours produced by the different analytes can be overcome by using specially designed urine test-strip readers. Less easily overcome, however, are the difficulties associated with the interpretation of unexpected findings, the numbers of which increase the more tests that are performed.

> Up to ten different tests can be carried out as rapidly, simply and almost as cheaply as just one or two

Some authors, including myself, are inclined to the view that despite its feasibility, urine should not be tested indiscriminately; instead, tests should be chosen for their potential usefulness. In other words, the test result should be meaningful within the context of the patient's illness or, when used as a screening procedure, do less harm than good.

Whilst some analyses, e.g. protein, glucose, and possibly haemoglobin, should probably be performed on all admissions to hospital, or on a patient's first attendance at a doctor's office for a new complaint, few other tests meet these criteria. A recent survey of urinalysis practice, for example, showed that most laboratories responding to a postal questionnaire[3] placed great score by urinary pH measurements – though it is difficult to understand why!

In urinalysis, as with all procedures, the clinician should, on the basis of his knowledge and understanding of the patient's illness, decide what tests are appropriate. These will often include microscopy for red and white cells, casts and bacteria[3], even though chemical tests purporting to give the same information are readily available[4].

Awareness of the need for attention to detail in the collection, storage and transportation of specimens, quality assurance, and a requirement for at least a modicum of training for operatives, has accompanied the introduction of "Near Patient Testing" using blood[5].

Application of the same principles to urine analysis will undoubtedly lead to a greater appreciation of its value in well defined situations, to the benefit of patients and doctors alike – not to mention those who pay the bills.

### References

1. Campbell, I., Gosling, P. Pre-operative screening; routine urine testing is good enough in patients under 50. Brit.Med.J. (1988); **297**: 803–804.

2. Editorial – Is routine urinalysis worthwhile? Lancet (1988); **1**: 747.

3. Editorial – Summary of Labmedica urinalysis questionnaires. Labmedica (1988); June/July, pp 18–19.

4. Arm, J.P., Peile, E.B., Rainford, D.J., et al. Significance of dipstick haematuria. 1. Correlation with microscopy of the urine. Brit.J.Urol. (1986); **58**: 211–217.

5. Marks, V. Essential considerations in the provision of near patient testing. Ann.Clin.Biochem. (1988); **25**: 220–225.

# Formation and Physical Characteristics of Urine

**Dr. G. Walker**

Chemical Pathologist, University Hospital, Nottingham

Urine is formed by the kidneys, and is the vehicle by which water and solutes in excess of body requirements are excreted, together with numerous end-products of metabolism, as well as foreign substances, including drugs and their metabolites. In health, the composition of urine varies according to the need to conserve or eliminate particular solutes. The detection of solutes not present in health, but found in a wide range of kidney and other diseases, justifies routine testing as part of the examination of patients, irrespective of their presenting complaint.

*The detection of solutes not present in health, but found in a wide range of diseases, justifies routine testing*

### Kidney Structure

The substance of a kidney consists of an ordered arrangement of approximately one million urine-forming units known as nephrons, associated with collecting ducts, blood vessels, lymphatics and nerves, bound together with a small amount of connective tissue.

Each nephron consists of a glomerulus and a tubule (*Figure 1*). The glomerular capsule, which is formed by invagination of the blind proximal end of the tubule, accommodates a tuft of capillaries separated from the capsular cells by a basement membrane. Tubules are formed from a single layer of epithelial cells surrounding a lumen. Three segments – the proximal convoluted tubule, the loop of Henle, and the distal convoluted tubule – are distinguished according to morphology and function. The open distal end of a tubule is inserted into a collecting duct, through which urine escapes into a calyx and thence into the pelvis, ureter and bladder.

Macroscopically, kidney substance – as shown in *Figure 2* – consists of an outer cortex and an inner medulla. Glomeruli are found only in the cortex. Tubules attached to glomeruli in the outer part of the cortex are confined to the cortex, while those associated with glomeruli close to the cortico-medullary junction are found together with collecting ducts in the medulla.

### Blood Supply

Blood from small arteries derived from the renal artery enters glomeruli through afferent arterioles and leaves through efferent arterioles, to pass through a peritubular network of capillaries and thence through venules and small veins into the renal vein. In addition, small arteries originating from larger arteries at the cortico-medullary junction pass into the medulla. They supply blood to capillaries which surround the tubules and collecting ducts, the blood being returned through corresponding venules and veins to the renal vein. Blood flow through the medullary vessels is important in maintaining an osmotic gradient in the medulla, which is necessary for the absorption of water from the collecting ducts. In a healthy adult, the renal blood flow is approximately 1.2 litres per minute, representing about 20% of the cardiac output.

### Formation of Urine

*Urine consists of a modified ultrafiltrate of plasma*

Urine consists of a modified ultrafiltrate of plasma. The ultrafiltrate is formed in the glomeruli and its volume and composition are modified as it passes through the tubules. Control mechanisms ensure that, in health, the composition of urine is appropriate to maintain the correct body content of water and of certain solutes – including sodium, potassium, calcium and phosphate.

Figure 1
Structural Relationships of the Nephron

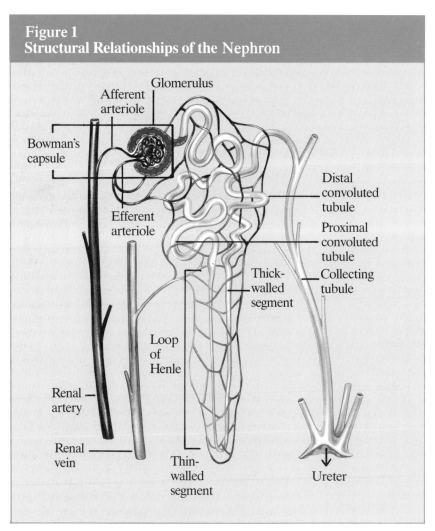

Figure 1
Structural Relationships of the Nephron

Glomerulus
Afferent arteriole
Bowman's capsule
Efferent arteriole
Renal artery
Renal vein
Distal convoluted tubule
Proximal convoluted tubule
Collecting tubule
Thick-walled segment
Loop of Henle
Thin-walled segment
Ureter

### Formation of the Glomerular Filtrate

Ultrafiltration depends primarily on the pressure of blood in the glomerular capillaries, which in turn depends on the arterial blood pressure and the resistance offered to blood flow by the afferent and efferent arterioles. In a healthy adult, the rate of ultrafiltration in the two kidneys – i.e. the glomerular filtration rate – depends on body mass, but is of the order of 120 ml per minute, representing 20% of the plasma passing through the glomeruli.

*Some proteins may appear in the glomerular filtrate as a result of glomerular damage*

Small molecules such as glucose, urea, amino acids, conjugated bilirubin and acetoacetate, pass freely from plasma into glomerular filtrate but, in health, most proteins – being large molecules – are almost completely excluded. However, in disease affecting glomeruli, changes in basement membrane structure and charge allow the passage of some proteins. In general, the more severe the changes, the larger the size of proteins appearing in the filtrate. Destruction of nephrons is a feature of many types of kidney disease, and results in a reduction of the glomerular filtration rate.

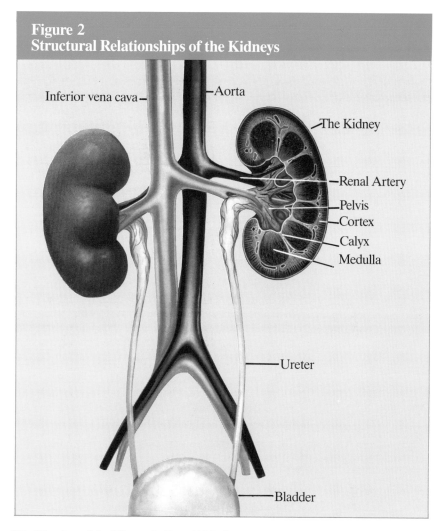

**Figure 2**
**Structural Relationships of the Kidneys**

Inferior vena cava

Aorta

The Kidney

Renal Artery

Pelvis

Cortex

Calyx

Medulla

Ureter

Bladder

### Modification of the Filtrate in Renal Tubules

Glomerular filtrate is modified and converted to urine by reabsorption of water and many solutes and, in the case of some solutes, by secretion into the lumen by cells of the tubules. In health, the volume and sodium and chloride contents of the filtrate are reduced by approximately 80% in the proximal tubules, while virtually all the glucose, amino acids and potassium are reabsorbed in this segment of the tubules. Additional chloride, together with sodium, is reabsorbed in the loop of Henle, while sodium is absorbed from the distal convoluted tubules in exchange for potassium and hydrogen ions – a process modulated by aldosterone, which is secreted by zona glomerulosa cells of the adrenal cortex in response to the need to conserve sodium. Most of the water leaving the distal convoluted tubules is reabsorbed from the collecting ducts. The amount depends on the osmotic activity of the medullary interstitium and on the permeability of the ducts – which is regulated by anti-diuretic hormone released from the neurohypophysis (posterior pituitary) in response to an increase in the effective osmolality of plasma. The renal handling of phosphate is also subject to hormonal regulation, tubular reabsorption being blocked by parathyroid hormone. Urate is mostly reabsorbed in the proximal convoluted tubules, while most of that appearing in the urine is secreted into the lumen of the distal convoluted tubules. The reabsorption of urea depends on the rate of formation of urine, being greatest at low rates. Creatinine is freely filtered through the glomeruli and, as there is very little exchange across tubular cells, measurement of endogenous creatinine clearance provides a convenient and, within limits, a useful means of determining glomerular filtration rate.

In health, urine is free of glucose because of complete reabsorption from the glomerular filtrate in the proximal convoluted tubules. However, when the plasma glucose level is raised, as in diabetes mellitus, more glucose than usual appears in the filtrate and, if above a critical level, exceeds the reabsorptive capacity of at least some tubules, so that some appears in the urine.

## PHYSICAL CHARACTERISTICS OF URINE

### Appearance

Abnormal urine colour may be due to the excretion of endogenous pigments, or drugs and their metabolites

The typical yellow colour of urine is due to a number of pigments, some – including riboflavine – derived from food, and others produced endogenously. In health, the intensity of colour varies with the rate of production, so that at high flow rates urine is pale, while at low flow rates it is more highly coloured. In disease, the colour of urine may be abnormal because of excretion of endogenous pigments as well as drugs and their metabolites (*Table 1*).

Urine which is clear when voided may become turbid on standing with, or without, the formation of a deposit of phosphate (soluble in acetic acid), oxalate (soluble in mineral acid), or urate (dissolves on heating). These substances are present in urine in health, but may be present in excess in disease states.

The urine of patients with urinary tract infections is often turbid

The urine of patients with pyogenic urinary tract infections is often turbid on voiding.

### Odour

The urine of patients with infection of the urinary tract with urea-splitting organisms smells of ammonia, while that of patients in diabetic ketoacidosis smells of acetone. Many inborn errors of metabolism, including phenylketonuria, maple syrup urine disease, isovaleric acidaemia and methionine malabsorption, result in the excretion of substances which give urine a characteristic odour.

### Volume

The rate of urine formation normally varies with fluid intake and extra-renal losses, and is appropriate to the maintenance of water homeostasis. A diurnal rhythm of excretion also operates, so that excess water is excreted more readily by day than at night. A minimum or "obligatory" volume of urine is excreted during fluid deprivation. This depends on the amount of solute excreted as well as antidiuretic hormone release, and the renal tubular response to it. In young adults the obligatory volume is 400–500 ml/day, but this increases with age. In certain diseases, water excretion is inappropriate to homeostatic needs. Impaired excretion occurs when renal perfusion is inadequate and/or renal

## Table 1
## Factors Affecting the Colour of Urine

| FACTOR | APPEARANCE |
|---|---|
| 1. **Endogenous** | |
| Conjugated Bilirubin | Yellow with yellow tinge to the froth when shaken |
| Haemoglobin, myoglobin and their oxidation products. | Red-brown |
| Intact erythrocytes. | "Smokey" red appearance |
| Urine may change colour on standing due to: | |
|     porphyrin precursors | Red |
|     melanogen(s) | Brown or black |
|     homogentisic acid | Brown or black (especially when the urine is alkaline) |
| Indican | Green or blue |
| 2. **Exogenous** | |
| Anthocyanins | Red urine after eating beetroot |
| Anthroquinones in laxatives, including senna, cascara and danthron | Orange |
| Mepacrine | Yellow |
| Methylene blue | Green |
| Phenolphthalein | Pink when alkaline |
| Rifampicin and phenazopyridine | Orange |
| L-dopa and sometimes in paracetamol poisoning | Becomes brown on standing |

function is grossly impaired by severe urinary tract obstruction, or in acute renal failure. Impaired renal conservation of water occurs:

– During osmotic diuresis, for instance in uncontrolled diabetes mellitus

– When the number of nephrons is reduced in chronic renal failure

– During recovery from acute renal failure

– In diabetes insipidus

– With hypercalcaemia

– With potassium depletion

– With certain inherited tubular defects.

### Specific Gravity and Osmolality

These are indices of total solute concentration. Specific gravity depends on the mass of individual solutes present per unit volume of solution, while osmolality depends on the total particle concentration, irrespective of the mass of individual particles. In complex solutions such as urine, there is only a very general relationship between specific gravity and osmolality.

In healthy young adults, urine specific gravity varies within the range 1.002–1.035, and osmolality between 50 and 1300 mmol/kg. The lowest values are found with very pale urine formed during maximal water diuresis, and the highest with highly concentrated urine formed in response to water deprivation. Young children and old people are unable to concentrate their urine as efficiently as young adults. Characteristic findings for urine SG in illness are listed in *Table 2*.

## Table 2
## Characteristic Findings for Urine Specific Gravity in Illness

**SG less than 1.010**

| | | |
|---|---|---|
| Polyuria | High fluid intake | Therapeutic Psychogenic polydipsia |
| | Diabetes insipidus | |
| | Antidiuretic hormone (ADH) resistance | Hypercalcaemia Hypokalaemia Lithium toxicity Rare inborn and acquired defects of renal tubular function |

**SG fixed at approximately 1.010**

| | |
|---|---|
| Oliguria | Acute renal failure |
| Polyuria | Polyuric acute renal failure including recovery from oliguric failure Chronic renal failure Heavy osmotic diuresis |

**SG greater than 1.025 in adults with intact urine concentrating mechanisms**

| | |
|---|---|
| Oliguria | Dehydration due to extra-renal water loss Post-injury or after surgery |
| Variable urine volume | Radiological contrast media for intravenous urography or angiography |

Specific gravity is easily measured, but measurement of osmolality in the laboratory is usually preferred for the assessment of patients with disorders of hydration and for the differential diagnosis of oliguria. In these conditions, it is important to consider the osmolality of urine in relation to that of plasma or serum. Typical findings are shown in *Table 3*.

Traditionally, SG has been measured on the wards using glass hydrometers ("urinometers"), which require relatively large volumes of sample, and are easily broken. A chemical, reagent strip method is now available, which changes colour according to the specific gravity. Changes in the ionic concentration of the sample are linked to a pH indicator system and the

## Table 3
## Urine and Plasma Osmolality in Disease

| | | Plasma (or serum) | Urine : Plasma (or serum) |
|---|---|---|---|
| **Oliguria** | | | |
| | Dehydration | High | U>P |
| | Acute renal failure | High | U≈P |
| | Post-injury | Variable | U>P |
| **Polyuria** | | | |
| | Diabetes insipidus and ADH resistance | High | U<P |
| | Psychogenic polydipsia | Low–normal | U<P |
| | Osmotic diuresis | High | U→P |
| | Chronic renal failure | Variable | U→P |
| | Recovery from acute renal failure | Variable | U→P |
| | Inappropriate secretion of ADH | Low | U>P |

The SG strip may give information which augments other reagent strip test results

readings are calibrated in terms of SG. This test is available on multiple reagent strips such as MULTISTIX* 8SG and MULTISTIX *10SG. The strip test has been shown to correlate with results obtained by the more traditional methods[1,2,3]; moreover, it is not affected by non-ionising solutes such as glucose and urea. It also gives information which may complement other reagent strip results, e.g. protein.

The SG strip test is useful in the management of urinary tract stone forming patients

Because it is so easily measured, urine specific gravity is particularly useful in the management of patients at risk of urinary tract stone formation, to monitor compliance with advice to maintain a high fluid intake, especially during hot weather.

### pH

In healthy adults, urine pH varies within the range 4.5–8.0. Values are usually lowest after an overnight fast and highest after meals. Urine pH is low in acidaemia, except when due to renal tubular acidosis, and high in alkalaemia, except when due to potassium depletion.

High pH values may be encountered in urine infected with urea-splitting organisms

Sodium bicarbonate and citrate are given to make urine alkaline, to reduce the risk of urinary stone formation in patients with cystinuria or hyperuricaemia. Urine pH measurements are made in these patients to check compliance and to adjust the dose. Spuriously low values for pH are seen when urine is collected into bottles containing acid preservative. High, frequently supra-physiological values, associated with a smell of ammonia, are encountered in urine infected with urea-splitting organisms.

**References**

1. Taylor, A., Walker, G. Novel method for measuring specific gravity of urine. Lancet (1982); **2**: 775.

2. Frew, A.J., et al. Estimation of urine specific gravity and osmolality using a simple reagent strip. Brit.Med.J. (1982); **285**: 1168.

3. Gounden, D., Newall, R.G. Urine specific gravity measurements: comparison of a new reagent strip method with existing methodologies as applied to the water concentration/dilution test. Curr.Med.Res.Op., (1983); **8**: 375.

# Glycosuria and Ketonuria

**R.W. Bilous**
Senior Registrar in Diabetes and Endocrinology
Newcastle upon Tyne

**K.G.M.M. Alberti**
Professor of Medicine
Newcastle upon Tyne

## GLYCOSURIA

### Definitions

Glycosuria is almost always the result of a raised blood glucose (hyperglycaemia). There are many medical conditions which are associated with hyperglycaemia, of which the commonest are diabetes mellitus and impaired glucose tolerance.

### Diabetes Mellitus and Impaired Glucose Tolerance

A random blood glucose of >10 mmol/L on venous plasma, or >11 mmol/L, capillary whole blood, on more than one occasion is diagnostic, as is a fasting venous blood (plasma) glucose equal to or more than 6.7 (7.8) mmol/L on two occasions. Equivocal cases require a 75g oral glucose tolerance test (OGTT). WHO has defined cut-off points for the diagnosis of diabetes with an OGTT; an intermediate at-risk category of impaired glucose tolerance (IGT) is also now recognised (*Table 1*).

---

**Table 1**
**Diagnostic Glucose Values Following a 75g Oral Glucose Tolerance Test**

The glucose load should be equivalent to 75g anhydrous glucose and taken over 5 minutes in 300–400ml water after an overnight fast, with the subject in the sitting position. At least two abnormal results are required (e.g. fasting and 2 hour, or 1 hour–2 hour and 2 hour) for the diagnosis of diabetes for clinical purposes in asymptomatic subjects.

| | Venous whole blood mmol/L (mg/dl) | Capillary whole blood mmol/L (mg/dl) | Venous plasma mmol/L (mg/dl) |
|---|---|---|---|
| **Diabetes Mellitus** | | | |
| Fasting | >6.7 (120) | >6.7 (120) | >7.8 (140) |
| 2 hours post load | >10.0 (180) | >11.1 (200) | >11.1 (200) |
| **Impaired Glucose Tolerance (IGT)** | | | |
| Fasting | <6.7 (120) | <6.7 (120) | <7.8 (140) |
| 2 hours post load | 6.7–9.9 (120–180) | 7.8–11.0 (140–200) | 7.8–11.0 (140–200) |
| **Normal** | | | |
| Fasting | <6.7 (120) | <6.7 (120) | <7.8 (140) |
| 2 hours post load | <6.7 (120) | <7.8 (140) | <7.8 (140) |

---

The prevalence of
diabetes in the UK is
between 0.5 and 2% for
the whole population

About one-half of
NIDDM subjects are
probably unrecognised

The prevalence of diabetes in the UK is approximately 0.2% in those under 20 years of age, and between 0.5 and 2.0% for the whole population; and the respective incidence rates are 0.1 and 1.5 per 1000 per annum. Between 10 and 20% are insulin-dependent (IDDM), the remainder being non insulin-dependent (NIDDM). Prevalence rates rise sharply with age from 45 years upwards, with an estimated 10–20% of the elderly being affected, and there is also an increased prevalence in certain racial groups, e.g. Asian Indians. About one-half of NIDDM subjects are probably unrecognised. Some of the rather sparse UK data on prevalence are summarised in *Table 2*.

## Table 2
## Incidence and Prevalence of Known Diabetes in the U.K.

a) **Incidence**

| IDDM | Age group (Years) | Corrected annual incidence (per 100,000) |
|---|---|---|
| | 0– 4 | 7.1 |
| | 5– 9 | 11.4 |
| | 10–14 | 20.0 |
| | 15–18 | 17.5 |

b) **Prevalence in whole population**

| | | Prevalence % |
|---|---|---|
| *Insulin treated* | Oxford | 0.38 |
| | Poole | 0.39 |
| | Southall | 0.33 |
| *Total* | Oxford | 1.1 |
| | Poole | 1.0 |
| | Southall: Caucasians | 1.2 |
| | : Asians | 2.2 |
| | : Afro-Caribbeans | 1.2 |
| | †Coventry (over 20 years) | |
| | : Caucasian | 2.8 males<br>4.3 females |
| | : Asians | 11.2 males<br>8.9 females |

†Population screening used.

### Other Causes of Hyperglycaemia

These are listed in the WHO Study Group report (1985) (*Table 3*).

*Cushing's syndrome:* cortisol increases hepatic glucose production (gluconeogenesis) in the long-term, and also opposes the peripheral actions of insulin.

*Acromegaly:* growth hormone over-production leads to IGT and diabetes in one-half or more of patients. This results in insulin antagonism in peripheral tissues, and long-term increases in gluconeogenesis.

**Table 3**
**Clinical Classification of Diabetes Mellitus and Glucose Intolerance (adapted from Ref. 2)**

1. *Diabetes mellitus*

   Insulin-dependent

   Non insulin-dependent      a) Non-obese
        b) Obese

   Malnutrition-related
   Other types associated with certain
   conditions and syndromes:

        1) pancreatic disease
        2) endocrinopathies
        3) drug or chemical induced
        4) abnormalities of insulin
           or its receptors
        5) genetic
        6) miscellaneous

2. *Impaired glucose tolerance*

   a) Non-obese
   b) Obese
   c) Associated with other
       conditions

3. *Gestational diabetes mellitus*

*Phaeochromocytoma:* catecholamines cause an increase in hepatic glucose production through both glycogen breakdown (glycogenolysis) and enhanced gluconeogenesis. They also prevent peripheral glucose uptake and suppress insulin release.

*Thyrotoxicosis:* hyperglycaemia and glycosuria can occasionally occur in thyrotoxic patients secondary to a combination of enhanced gluconeogenesis and increased insulin breakdown.

*Glucagonoma:* extremely rare. Over-production of glucagon by a pancreatic tumour can produce diabetes secondary to increased glycogenolysis and gluconeogenesis.

*Major trauma, stroke, myocardial infarction or circulatory collapse:* transient hyperglycaemia may occur in any of these circumstances, and may be secondary to catecholamine release. *N.B.* These conditions may also unmask hitherto unrecognised NIDDM.

*Iatrogenic:* oral steroid therapy has already been mentioned. Oestrogens displace cortisol from its binding, and through this and other mechanisms can cause mild hyperglycaemia. Long-term thiazide diuretic therapy can lead to reversible IGT, glycosuria or NIDDM in those with preceding IGT, but the precise mechanism is unclear. These drugs should be avoided in diabetic patients.

## CAUSES OF GLYCOSURIA

Glycosuria is usually
secondary to
hyperglycaemia

Urinalysis for glucose can
be a valuable method of
monitoring the disease in
some patients

Urine testing continues
to have a role
in the management of
the elderly

Glucose is a small molecule which is freely filtered at the renal glomerulus. In health, the proximal tubule reabsorbs all of the filtered glucose by an active process which has an upper rate limit or transport maximum or $T_M$. The $T_M$ for glucose is 10–14mmol/min/$1\cdot73m^2$ in normal man, which corresponds to a plasma glucose of 9–10mmol/L (180 mg/dl). Some individuals have a lower $T_M$ for glucose ($T_{MG}$) and will have demonstrable glycosuria at normal or only slightly increased blood glucose concentrations. Such people are said to have a low renal threshold for glucose, and this phenomenon is often called renal glycosuria. Glycosuria can also occur as a result of renal tubular disorders such as acute tubular necrosis or the very rare Fanconi syndrome. It can also occur in otherwise normal pregnancy, probably as a result of an increased glomerular filtration of glucose, but in the overwhelming majority of cases glycosuria is secondary to hyperglycaemia.

Once a diagnosis of diabetes is made, urinalysis for glucose can be a valuable method of monitoring the disease in some patients. It is now generally accepted that the microvascular complications of diabetes affecting the eye, kidney and peripheral nerve are secondary to prolonged hyperglycaemia, and that glycaemic correction to normal or near-normal values should be a primary objective of diabetic care. However, the major risk of this treatment strategy, particularly in the insulin-treated patient, is that of hypoglycaemia, which cannot be detected by urinalysis for glucose. The development of easy to use methods for capillary blood glucose monitoring has, however, meant that blood testing – particularly for those on insulin therapy – has superseded urinalysis in diabetes management for many patients. Urine testing continues to have a role, however, in the management of the elderly – in whom the symptomatic relief from hyperglycaemia is the main objective – and in those patients who cannot perform capillary blood sampling for whatever reason. In these cases, early morning fasting and 1–2 hour post main meal specimens, once to three times weekly are probably adequate.

## GROUPS AT RISK FOR DIABETES

Before discussing screening for diabetes, it is useful to identify any individuals at particular risk of developing the disease. This allows consideration of selective screening, and such individuals would include the elderly, those women with a previous history of gestational diabetes, those who are obese (body mass index >30), those with a strong family history of diabetes, those with premature macrovascular disease and those with chronic infections.

## SCREENING FOR DIABETES

It should be stressed that all diabetic patients – whether on diet, tablets or insulin – are prone to microvascular complications, and patients with IGT have an increased incidence of macrovascular disease. In addition, the older patient may have had relatively asymptomatic, modest hyperglycaemia for many years prior to presentation, particularly if he or she has a high renal threshold for glucose, and about 20% have established retinopathy at the time of diagnosis. Thus the early detection of these patients is important, and it is possible to make a strong case for screening selected populations for diabetes, particularly the middle aged and elderly. Urine testing for glucose is the most widely used test because of its simplicity and specificity, but blood glucose assessment is preferable, as it is more specific and sensitive, and should be used if blood is being taken for other purposes.

Routine urinalysis for glucose should be performed on all hospital admissions, in all pregnant women at each antenatal clinic attendance, and in all patients having a general medical check-up. Elderly patients, especially if they are taking thiazide diuretics, should be tested regularly, perhaps annually. Individuals who are obese, who have documented hyperlipidaemia or gout, who are hypertensive or who have recurrent skin or urinary tract infections, or who have a history of previous pancreatic disease or gestational diabetes, should also be tested regularly. Whether widespread whole population screening should be undertaken is not yet clear. Certainly, community-based surveys detect many previously undiagnosed diabetic patients, but the cost benefits of screening the entire UK population have not been defined, and it should probably not be undertaken until the treatment of NIDDM is more effective than at present. Nonetheless, if a screening procedure is being performed for other reasons, e.g. medicals at work, cervical screening, or cardiovascular screening, then the incorporation of urinalysis for glucose is almost certainly justified. *Table 4* summarises the groups who should be screened.

---

**Table 4
Groups to be Screened for Diabetes**

- All hospital admissions
- All patients having a general medical check-up
- Elderly
- Pregnant women – at each clinic visit
- Women with history of gestational diabetes
- Family history of diabetes
- Obese
- Hyperlipidaemics
- Patients with gout
- Hypertensives
- Chronic infections
- Premature macrovascular disease
- History of pancreatic disease

---

**METHODS FOR THE RAPID MEASUREMENT OF URINE GLUCOSE**

There are two broad categories of urine test for glucose: reduction tests incorporating the principles of Benedict's test for reducing substances (CLINITEST*); and the enzymatic tests which use glucose oxidase-impregnated test strips and are thus glucose specific (e.g. CLINISTIX*, DIASTIX*, Diabur 5000™, and multiple strips).

## 1. Reduction tests

CLINITEST tablets contain anhydrous copper sulphate, sodium hydroxide, anhydrous citric acid and anhydrous sodium carbonate. Five drops of urine and ten drops of water are pipetted into a test tube and a CLINITEST tablet is dropped in. Hydration generates heat which boils the mixture. Fifteen seconds after the reaction subsides, the tube is gently shaken and the colour of the solution compared to a colour chart, ranging from blue (negative) to bright orange (2%, 111 mmol/L). This test is sensitive only to concentrations >14mmol/L (¼%), but its upper limit of accuracy can be increased to 5% (280 mmol/L) using only two drops of urine and a special colour chart.

CLINITEST is not specific for glucose (see below), and is also slightly cumbersome to perform. The tablets have a finite shelf life, they are caustic and dangerous if ingested, and should be stored in air-tight, child-proof containers. For these reasons, many patients now use the much more convenient enzymatic test strips. One important remaining indication for CLINITEST is in neonates, who should have a test performed to detect the rare but serious condition of galactosaemia. Such infants test positive with CLINITEST but negative with an enzymatic test strip.

*Neonates should be tested with CLINITEST to detect the rare but serious condition of galactosaemia*

## 2. Enzymatic Methods

These tests involve two sequential reactions, and are performed by either dipping the strip into an aliquot of urine or holding it in the urine stream.

a) Glucose is oxidised by glucose oxidase to form gluconic acid and hydrogen peroxide.

$$\text{Glucose} + O_2 + H_2O \xrightarrow{\text{Glucose Oxidase}} \text{Gluconic acid} + H_2O_2$$

b) The peroxide, in the presence of peroxidase, reacts with a colourless chromogen (either o-tolidine, potassium iodide or tetramethylbenzidine), which is then oxidised to a coloured marker; green to brown (DIASTIX, Ames multiple strips), purple to violet (CLINISTIX) or yellow to dark green (BM combination strips). Diabur 5000 strips incorporate two reagent areas with different sensitivities to glucose. All of these enzymatic strips can detect glucose concentrations of 0.1% (5.5 mmol/L) to 2% (111 mmol/L), or 5% (280 mmol/L, Diabur 5000 only). Reading times range from 10 seconds (CLINISTIX) to two minutes (Diabur 5000).

The CLINISTIX test is qualitative only, and in our opinion probably should no longer be used for day to day monitoring; it is still, of course, adequate for screening purposes. The other strips are semi-quantitative only because other urinary chromogens can interfere with the final colour. However, concordance in the region of 75% between strip test results and laboratory estimation has been reported.

## 3. False Negative and False Positive Results

Because the enzymatic methods are chemically specific and quite sensitive, false negative and positive results are unusual (*Table 5*). CLINITEST, however, will be positive for any reducing agent and has a higher false positive rate. It is important to remember that bacteria will metabolise glucose, so that specimens allowed to stand for several hours at room temperature may test negative. Hyperglycaemic patients with severely reduced glomerular filtration rates may fail to demonstrate glycosuria if their $T_{MG}$ is not exceeded. These two examples, of course, represent true negative results chemically, although misleading clinically.

**Table 5**
**Causes of False Negative and False Positive Reactions for Glucose**

| Reduction Methods | | Enzymatic Methods | |
|---|---|---|---|
| CLINITEST | CLINISTIX | DIASTIX/ Multiple strips | Diabur 5000 |
| *False negative reactions* | | | |
| Tablet deterioration | Vitamin C | Vitamin C (high levels) | Vitamin C |
| | Salicylates | Salicylates (massive doses) | Salicylates |
| – | L-Dopa | L-Dopa | L-Dopa |
| – | High specific gravity | – | – |
| – | – | High concentrations of ketones | – |
| *False positive reactions* | | | |
| Other reducing sugars | | All affected by detergents, peroxides and hypochlorite | |
| Lactose Fructose Galactose Pentose | | | |
| Drugs: Aspirin Vitamin C Tetracycline L-Dopa Nalidixic acid Probenecid Cephalosporins (black colour) | | | |

## CLINITEST:

*False negative results* are rare. Exposure to moisture turns the hydrophilic tablets dark blue or black; if this occurs they should be discarded.

*False positive results* are more common and occur with any of the following reducing sugars:

i) Lactose, excreted in late pregnancy and lactation

ii) Fructose, following consumption of large quantities of fruit or confectionery. It is also present in the rare but benign essential fructosuria, and the more serious condition of fructose intolerance which causes severe hypoglycaemia in infancy.

iii) Galactose is present in the urine of infants with galactosaemia, and its reaction with CLINITEST is used as the basis for neonatal screening.

iv) Pentose sugars occur rarely and are of no significance.

v) Drugs such as aspirin which are conjugated to glucuronic acid develop reducing properties; others, such as vitamin C, tetracyclines, L-dopa metabolites, nalidixic acid and probenecid may also give false positive test results. Some first-generation cephalosporins can produce a black colour, but later preparations do not have this property.

### Enzymatic Tests

*False negative results* can occur if there are large amounts of vitamin C present, such as in proprietary vitamin supplements or some tetracycline preparations in which it is used as a preservative. Other drugs such as metabolites of L-dopa may suppress colour development. CLINISTIX strips are affected by a high urine specific gravity which will decrease sensitivity, and DIASTIX and multiple strips (but not Diabur 5000 or CLINISTIX) have a similar problem when high concentrations of ketone bodies are present.

*False positive results* are extremely rare, and only occur if the urine container has been accidentally contaminated with detergents, hypochlorite or peroxides.

### 4. Choice of Test

Obviously it is sensible to use those tests which are both sensitive and specific, easiest to perform, least susceptible to manipulative error and least open to interferences. It seems evident, therefore, that the two most modern test strips fit these criteria (DIASTIX, Diabur 5000) and should be used in most circumstances. When several tests on urine are required, then the equivalent multiple strip should be used.

### 5. Quality Assurance

All chemical tests performed in laboratories are subject to rigorous quality control procedures. By contrast, little or no quality assurance is applied to extra-laboratory tests. This applies most specifically to urine tests, which are often performed by untrained junior medical personnel. Errors are common and generally go undetected. At a minimum, whenever a new bottle of test strips are opened, or if the strips have not been used for some time, then the first strip should be dipped into a standard test solution, such as CHEK-STIX*.

A wall chart should be kept and appropriate instructions given for action to be taken when inaccurate results are obtained. All personnel using test strips should be trained by skilled individuals. Unannounced spot checks of all staff performing these tests should be carried out periodically on wards and in outpatient clinics. No satisfactory system of quality assurance of patient urine tests has yet been devised.

### 6. Interpretation of Results and Action to be Taken

If the glycosuric patient has symptoms of thirst and polyuria, then they are likely to have diabetes and blood glucose levels should be measured. This is readily and quickly determined using a test strip and capillary blood. If the symptoms are severe, the patient is young (<35 years) or there is marked ketonuria, then urgent hospital referral is necessary.

In the asymptomatic person, a second blood glucose measurement should be performed to confirm the diagnosis (see *Table 1*).

Only if the blood glucose value is <11 mmol/L should a formal oral glucose tolerance test be considered. Once the diagnosis of diabetes is confirmed, then it is important that all patients have a careful examination of eyes, feet (to detect possible neuropathy and ischaemia), and measurement of blood pressure, lipids and microalbuminuria. All diabetic patients need regular, careful review, at time intervals appropriate to their age and medical condition. There is no evidence to show that specific hypoglycaemic therapy confers any benefit on patients with IGT, although a small percentage will progress to frank diabetes each year.

*Persistent heavy glycosuria in known diabetic patients with a normal renal threshold suggests sub-optimal treatment*

Persistent heavy glycosuria in known diabetic patients with a normal renal threshold suggests sub-optimal treatment, particularly if there is concurrent weight loss. Such patients need urgent review for optimisation of diabetic treatment and possible transfer to insulin therapy. In those rare patients with false positive CLINITEST and a true negative enzymatic test, detailed chemical examination of their urine will determine the nature of the reducing substance present. This testing is much more urgent in the neonate than in the adult patient.

## KETONURIA

### CAUSES OF KETONURIA

Ketonuria occurs secondary to increased blood levels of the three so-called ketone bodies: acetoacetic acid, acetone and 3-hydroxybutyrate, and these increases occur following increased metabolism of body fat.

Fat is stored mainly as triglyceride and is derived from dietary intake. Insulin has a major role in lipogenesis and, together with glucagon, controls hepatic fatty acid metabolism.

In the fasting state, peripheral fatty acid is mobilised by local tissue lipase. Free fatty acids can be oxidised by all major tissues, and about 30% are taken up by the liver, where acetyl CoA is produced by a process called beta-oxidation. A proportion of the acetyl CoA condenses to form acetoacetate which, in turn, can be reduced to 3-hydroxybutyrate or decarboxylated to acetone. The ketone bodies provide a useful energy source for respiring muscle and nervous tissue (in the fasting state), and are freely filtered at the renal glomerulus. Acetone is largely excreted by the lungs, so the urine contains mainly 3-hydroxybutyrate (78%) and acetoacetate (20%).

In the insulin-deficient patient unrestrained fat breakdown occurs, with a consequent large rise in circulating free fatty acids and over-producion of ketone bodies. This produces a metabolic acidosis which can be lethal if left untreated. Raised blood and urine ketone levels also occur in starvation states such as prolonged fasting, extreme dieting, anorexia nervosa, gastro-intestinal disorders causing vomiting such as pyloric stenosis and hyperemesis gravidarum; but never to the extent seen in diabetic ketoacidosis. Ketonuria may also occur in patients suffering a febrile illness. Ketonuria occurs particularly rapidly in fasting children because of very limited glycogen stores.

The generation and control of ketone bodies is outlined in *Figure 1*.

### TESTS FOR KETONURIA

There are two types of tests, those using tablets as a modification of Rothera's test (ACETEST*) and those using test strips which are a modified Legal's test (KETOSTIX*, Ketur Test). Both types use the property of nitroprusside to form a purple colour with acetone and acetoacetic acid in the presence of alkali; neither will detect 3-hydroxybutyrate. Gerhardt's ferric chloride test is non-specific for acetoacetic acid and is no longer in routine use.

### ACETEST

An ACETEST tablet containing aminoacetic acid, sodium nitroprusside, phosphate and borate, is placed on a piece of white paper and one drop of urine (serum, plasma or whole blood) is placed on it. The urine test colour is compared with a colour chart after 30 seconds, 2 minutes for plasma or serum and 10 minutes for whole blood.

### KETOSTIX, Ketur-test

The test strips are dipped into a urine sample and the colour checked against the chart after 15–30 seconds. Both strips are much less sensitive to acetone, and should be regarded as almost specific for acetoacetic acid. Their lower limit for sensitivity is 0.5 mmol/L. Separated plasma and serum, but not whole blood, can also be tested with these strips.

#### False Negative and Positive Results

*False negative results* are uncommon with any of these tests, although ACETEST tablets can deteriorate if exposed to moisture. The depth of purple colour is a semi-quantitative assessment of the degree of ketoacidosis, but will underestimate severe cases when the contribution of 3-hydroxybutyrate may be very high.

*False positive results* have been reported in patients taking phthaleins, although the colour produced is red, not violet. A similar red colouration is found with phenylketones, which can be present in patients taking large quantities of L-dopa.

#### Interpretation of Results and Actions to be Taken

Marked ketonuria in a previously undiagnosed diabetic patient is an absolute indication for hospital referral. Persistent ketonuria in insulin-treated patients suggests under-insulinisation, and is an indication for urgent optimisation of

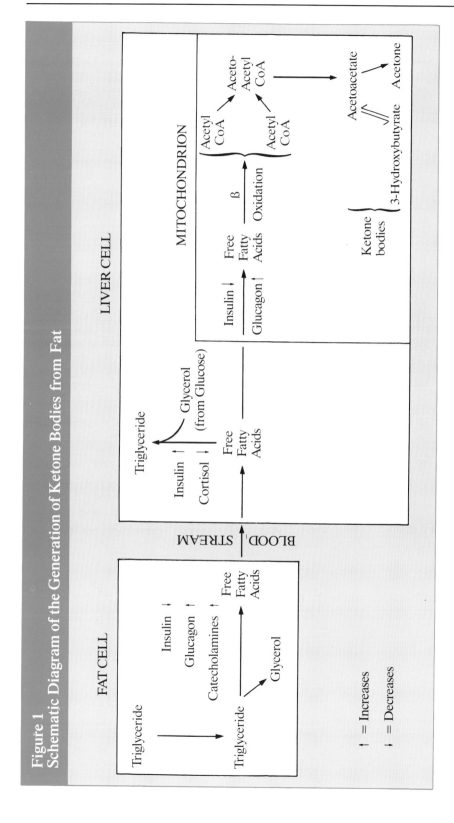

Figure 1
Schematic Diagram of the Generation of Ketone Bodies from Fat

Persistent ketonuria in insulin-treated patients suggests under-insulinisation and indicates urgent optimisation of treatment

treatment. The exception to this role is the pregnant insulin-dependent woman, who may develop such a low renal threshold for glucose that consequent heavy glycosuria with even near-normal blood glucose levels may produce "starvation ketosis". Such patients need more carbohydrate and not more insulin. There is a small group of insulin-dependent patients, usually young women, who show rapid and unpredictable swings of glycaemia and have repeated episodes of often life-threatening ketoacidosis (so called "brittle diabetes"). Such patients benefit from regular monitoring for ketonuria as a means of assessing their need for more insulin or hospitalisation. Monitoring ketonuria can also be useful in insulin-dependent patients undergoing an intercurrent illness such as gastroenteritis, although such patients ought to be referred if they are unable to take sufficient oral fluids. In the rare patient with a high renal threshold for glucose, measurement of ketonuria may be the first indication of insulin-deficiency, so it is important to test for both glucose and ketones in any newly presenting patient, or any diabetic patient who is unwell for an unknown reason. All young insulin-dependent diabetic patients should be equipped with ketone-testing strips or tablets for use during illness or periods of poor glycaemic control. Combined test strips for glucose and ketones are available, but not prescribable on form FP10. Both glucose and ketones are routinely tested on the multiple combination strips.

*It is important to test for both glucose and ketones in any newly presenting patient, or any diabetic patient who is unwell*

*All young insulin-dependent diabetic patients should be equipped with ketone-testing strips or tablets*

In the overweight patient, mild to moderate ketonuria is an indication of dietary adherence; its absence suggests non-compliance. Some non-insulin dependent diabetic patients may show moderate ketonuria at presentation, but this does not always imply ketoacidosis and is probably a consequence of relative under-insulinisation or possible anorexia. An urgent plasma bicarbonate determination will detect significant acidosis.

In the very ill patient, ketonuria implies significant fat breakdown, and dietary supplementation, by either the enteral or parenteral route is advisable.

## WHERE SHOULD RAPID URINE TESTING BE PERFORMED?

*Those performing urine testing should be adequately trained*

Urine glucose and ketone body tests can usefully be performed at all levels of health care: the home, primary healthcare centres, outpatient clinics and hospital wards. The only proviso is that those performing the tests should be adequately trained in their performance and interpretation of the results.

## BENEFITS OF RAPID URINE GLUCOSE AND KETONE TESTS

*Urine testing for glucose and ketones can avert serious illness and possibly avoid unnecessary hospitalisation and morbidity*

There are major benefits to the diabetic patient as an adjunct to self-monitoring and self-management. They serve as early warning systems for deterioration of diabetic control and, as such, can avert serious illness and possibly avoid unnecessary hospitalisation and morbidity. They are useful for opportunistic screening, and while they may not be as good as a blood test, they are both simpler to perform and cheaper.

### Further Reading

Hockaday, T.D.R, Alberti, K.G.M.M. Diabetes Mellitus. in: Oxford Textbook of Medicine, 2nd Edition, Weatherall, D.J., Ledingham, J.G.G., Warrell, D.A., Eds., Oxford University Press, Oxford 1987, pp.9.51–9.101.

WHO Study Group on diabetes mellitus, report. Technical Report Series 727. WHO, Geneva 1985.

# Haematuria

Wing Commander David J Rainford, MBE.
Consultant in Renal Medicine
Squadron Leader Nigel A Harrison
Senior Registrar
Princess Mary's Royal Air Force Hospital, Halton, Aylesbury

Haematuria literally means blood in the urine. It may either be macroscopic and therefore obvious, or microscopic and detectable only by chemical tests. It is important to note that disorders that cause haematuria may present in either manner.

## What is Normal?

*A few red cells in the urine are entirely normal*

A few red cells in the urine are entirely normal. This has been recognised for many years. Indeed, Addis[1] found up to 425 thousand red cells in the overnight urine of healthy people and suggested that up to one million red cells might be normal. As the average overnight urine volume was 352 ml, this gives an upper limit of normal of 2 to 3 red cells per microlitre. Addis used bright light microscopy, which is notorious for underestimating the number of red cells. The use of phase contrast microscopy on unspun urine has now shown that up to 8 red cells per microlitre may be regarded as normal[2]. Over that limit must be regarded as pathological.

## Prevalence

A population screening study of 10,050 adult males using LABSTIX* reagent strips showed a prevalence of haematuria of 2.5%[3]. The prevalence in children is about 1%[4].

## Causes of Haematuria

*In adult patients with haematuria where urological causes are excluded, the majority may have glomerular disease*

Blood may enter the urine at any point from the glomerulus to the external urethral meatus. A list of causes appears in *Table 1*. In adult patients where urological causes are excluded by careful assessment, the majority may be shown to have glomerular disease at renal biopsy[5].

Haematuria may occasionally occur in response to exercise. It is generally accepted that exercise-induced haematuria that resolves in 24-48 hours in an otherwise normal individual is entirely benign[6]. It is important, however, to remember that exercise-induced haematuria may indicate urinary tract pathology such as stones or glomerular nephritis[7].

## Detection of Haematuria

Whilst the passage of frank blood in the urine is dramatic and usually results in the patient seeking medical attention, the majority of patients with haematuria are discovered by chemical testing at routine health screening for employment or insurance purposes.

*The urine strip test for blood can reliably replace microscopy*

Routine phase contrast microscopy to distinguish the normal from the abnormal is clearly impractical, and reliance is therefore placed upon chemical testing using a reagent strip to make this distinction. Is this a valid substitute? It has now been shown that the urine strip test for blood is an efficient method and can reliably replace microscopy[8]. We evaluated N-MULTISTIX SG,

Consistently negative
strips excluded
significant haematuria

When patients with
one or more "trace" or
greater strip results
were investigated, a cause
for haematuria was
found in all patients

comparing it with red cell counts of unspun urine, and positive results were correlated with pathology. 24% of single negative results contained 10 or more red cells per microlitre, but consistently negative strips excluded significant haematuria. Single results greater than "trace" positive almost invariably indicated the presence of significant haematuria. 19% of "trace" positive results contained less than 10 red cells per microlitre. However, when patients with one or more positive strip results, even if only "trace" positive, were investigated, a cause for haematuria was found in all patients. The two commonest diagnoses were mesangial proliferative glomerular nephritis and inflammatory lesions of the lower urinary tract[7].

**Table 1**
**Causes of Haematuria**

| **General** | Bleeding disorders<br>Warfarin therapy |
|---|---|
| **Urological** | Trauma<br>Stones<br>Malignancy – hypernephroma<br>             prostate<br>             pelvis / ureter<br>             bladder<br>Benign prostatic hypertrophy<br>Renal infarction<br>Angioma<br>Bladder diverticulum<br>Urethral stricture<br>Endometriosis<br>Hunner's ulcer |
| **Nephrological** | Glomerular nephritis<br>Polycystic disease<br>Sickle cell disease/trait<br>Vasculitis<br>Collagen disorders<br>Loin pain/haematuria syndrome<br>Infections –   cystitis<br>             prostatitis<br>             urethritis<br>             tuberculosis<br>             schistosomiasis |

### The Reagent Strip

The chemical detection of blood in the urine using a reagent strip is based on the peroxidase-like activity of haemoglobin. This will catalyse the reaction of cumene hydroperoxide and 3,3′,5,5′ – tetramethyl benzidine, producing a blue colour on the strip. The test will therefore detect intact red cells, free haemoglobin and myoglobin, but false positive reactions may occur with oxidising agents and false negative reactions in the presence of reducing agents (see *Table 2*).

| Table 2 Factors Affecting the Reagent Strip Test for Blood | |
|---|---|
| **True Positive** | Red cells<br>Haemoglobin<br>Myoglobin |
| **False Positive** | Hypochlorite solutions<br>Oxidising agents<br>Bacterial peroxidase |
| **False Negative** | Vitamin C<br>Gentisic acid<br>Poorly mixed urine |

### Upper or Lower Tract Bleeding?

The use of phase contrast microscopy to examine the morphology of red cells in the urine has been recommended by some workers as a useful tool to differentiate upper from lower urinary tract bleeding[2]. The cells from glomerular bleeding are abnormal in shape, crenated or damaged. Those of lower urinary tract origin appear normal.

In its purest form the distinction is useful, but unfortunately often a mixture of cells is present and interpretation is difficult. With mesangial IgA disease – possibly the commonest cause of bleeding – red cell morphology is almost invariably a combination of upper and lower tract cells[9]. The presence of casts at microscopy is probably as good an indicator as any to the glomerular origin of the red cells.

Attempts to refine the identification of bleeding site and indeed the underlying pathology by measurement of red cell size distribution have been made using haematology counters such as the Coulter S.

> The combination of significant proteinuria with haematuria in the absence of infection is highly suggestive of renal pathology.

Testing for blood in the urine is rarely performed in isolation, and the combination of significant proteinuria with haematuria in the absence of infection is highly suggestive of renal pathology.

### The Management of Confirmed Haematuria

Whilst the subsequent investigation of adults and children will differ, initial management should be the same. A very full history should be taken in an attempt to identify the likely cause. Family history may suggest polycystic renal disease, sickle cell disease, bleeding disorders or a hereditary nephritis. Full clinical examination will help to exclude systemic diseases, tumour masses and abnormalities of the external genitalia.

### Children

The occurrence of haematuria in a child is usually a source of great anxiety to the parents. Often a good history and examination routine will allow reassurance without the need for major invasive investigation.

A history of frequency and dysuria will suggest an infective origin, loin pain without systemic symptoms the possibility of stone disease. Rashes, abdominal and joint pains all point to systemic disease such as Henoch-Schönlein Purpura. Association with upper respiratory infections will suggest Berger's disease as the culprit. On clinical examination, a mass in the loin may be found in association with Wilm's tumour, signs of salt and water retention with the acute nephritides.

In cases of isolated haematuria, a plain abdominal radiograph to exclude radio-opaque stones and an ultrasound scan for size, shape and position of the kidneys is usually all the imaging that is required. With kidneys of normal morphology, if the plasma creatinine and C3 complement are normal, the parents may be reassured and the child followed up at regular six-monthly intervals. If there is associated proteinuria, hypertension, reduced renal function or a low C3 complement, then the child should be referred to a paediatric nephrologist.

An excellent account of the investigation of haematuria in children has been written by Professor R.H.R. White, and the reader's attention is drawn to this for further information[10].

### Adults

Haematuria in the adult always gives rise to the concern that underlying malignancy may be responsible. Whilst most cases of bladder cancer occur after the age of forty years, the authors have seen several such cases in males in their late teens and early twenties. Previous studies of haematuria have shown an incidence of urinary tract malignancy of around 10%[11]. Full urological examination in cases of haematuria in the adult should be mandatory.

As in the child, a full history and examination is essential and may give important clues as to the cause of bleeding. A family history is occasionally present with focal nephritis and mesangiocapillary nephritis, and does not necessarily mean that the patient has so called "hereditary nephritis". This term is often used synonymously with Alport's syndrome. A family history of deafness or visual problems with nephritis would point to this as a diagnosis.

After excluding infection, the majority of cases of haematuria in the adult will be due to focal segmental nephritis

Despite the concerns over malignancy, after excluding infection, the majority of cases of haematuria in the adult will be due to focal segmental nephritis. The commonest of these is Mesangial IgA disease. In general terms, the prognosis for focal nephritis is excellent and only a small proportion of patients (approximately 13%) will develop severe renal disease.

A plan for investigation of the adult with haematuria appears in *Figure 1*.

The algorithm assumes that haematuria has been confirmed. Any history of frank haematuria, even with a negative urine subsequently, should receive full urological assessment, and so the plan is most appropriate to the discovery of microscopic haematuria. Although there is a trend now to substitute the IVU with ultrasound examination, the two should be considered complementary and

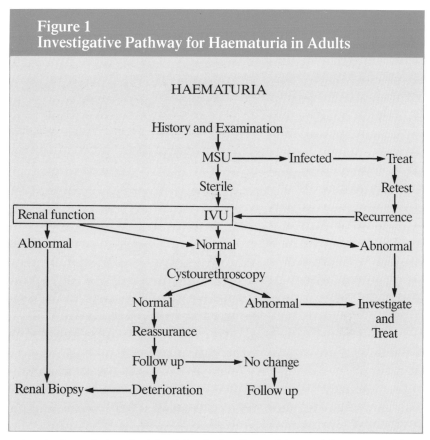

**Figure 1**
**Investigative Pathway for Haematuria in Adults**

HAEMATURIA

History and Examination

MSU ⟶ Infected ⟶ Treat

Sterile                    Retest

Renal function    IVU ⟵ Recurrence

Abnormal        Normal        Abnormal

Cystourethroscopy

Normal              Abnormal ⟶ Investigate and Treat

Reassurance

Follow up ⟶ No change

Renal Biopsy ⟵ Deterioration        Follow up

not mutually exclusive. A plain abdominal radiograph is certainly more sensitive for the diagnosis of small calculi. Pre- and post- micturition ultrasound scans are relatively sensitive in demonstrating even small bladder tumours.

After excluding urological causes, a renal biopsy should be considered in patients with haematuria if:

    a) Renal function is abnormal
    b) There is associated proteinuria
    c) There is a persistently low C3 complement level
    d) There is a suggestion of hereditary nephritis
    e) Systemic disease is present, e.g. SLE or vasculitis
    f) A firm diagnosis is required in the absence of (a) to (e) for insurance or employment purposes, or to allay anxiety in the patient or parents.

### Conclusion

*The presence of "1+" blood or greater always merits further investigation*

Haematuria is a serious warning of underlying disease and should not be ignored. The urinary reagent strip is extremely reliable as a guide to the presence of abnormal haematuria. The presence of "+" or greater strip results always merits further investigation.

In the absence of a urological cause and in the presence of a sterile urine, most cases will be due to an underlying glomerular nephritis. In general terms, the prognosis for isolated haematuria due to glomerular nephritis is good in the absence of associated proteinuria, hypertension or abnormal renal function.

## References

1. Addis, T. The number of formed elements in the urinary sediment of normal individuals. J.Clin.Invest. (1926); **2**: 409–415.

2. Fairley, K.A., Birch, D.F., Haematuria: a simple method for identifying glomerular bleeding. Kidney Int. (1982); **21**: 105–108.

3. Ritchie, C.D., Bevan, E.A., Collier, StJ. Importance of occult haematuria found at routine screening. Brit.Med.J. (1986); **292**: 681–683.

4. Lee, H., Haematuria. Focus on urine analysis. The Medicine Publishing Foundation, Oxford (1983); p20.

5. Burkholder, G.V., Dotin, L.N., Thomason, W.B., Beach, P.D. Unexplained haematuria. JAMA (1969); **210**: 1729–1733.

6. Kincaid-Smith, P. Haematuria and exercise-related haematuria. Brit.Med.J. (1982); **285**: 1595–1596.

7. Arm, J.P., Peile, E.B., Rainford, D.J. Significance of dipstick haematuria. 2. Correlation with pathology. Brit.J.Urol. (1986b); **58**: 211–217.

8. Arm, J.P., Peile, E.B., Rainford, D.J., Strike, P.W. and Tettmar, R.E. Significance of dipstick haematuria. 1. Correlation with microscopy of the urine. Brit.J.Urol. (1986a); **58**: 211–217.

9. Fasset, R.G., Horgan, B.A. and Mathew, T.H. Detection of glomerular bleeding by phase contrast microscopy. Lancet, (1982); **i**: 1432–1434.

10. White, R.H.R. The investigation of haematuria. Arch.Dis.Child (1989); **64**: 159–165.

11. Golin, A.L., Howard, R.S. Asymptomatic microscopic haematuria. J.Urol. (1980); **124**: 389–391.

# Proteinuria

**Squadron Leader Nigel A Harrison**
Senior Registrar
**Wing Commander David J Rainford, MBE**
Consultant in Renal Medicine

Renal Unit, Princess Mary's Royal Air Force Hospital,
Halton, Aylesbury

## INTRODUCTION

Isolated asymptomatic proteinuria is a common finding, especially at medical examinations. Its presence may have serious consequences for the individual's employability or insurability. When found in small amounts, it poses the question both as to its significance and the requirement for further investigation. In general, the prognosis for proteinuria depends on its degree, the pattern of excretion, and whether the urine deposit is otherwise normal.

### Mechanisms of Proteinuria

There are two main factors preventing the leakage of protein at the glomerular level – "sieve" size, and basement membrane charge. The glomerulus is basically a sieve, whose holes are of a size to prevent the egress of molecules greater than 33,000 Daltons molecular weight. Albumin has a molecular weight of 67,000 Daltons. What little albumin that does escape is rapidly reabsorbed by the tubules. The glomerular basement membrane is rich in negatively charged glycoproteins aligned along its endothelial side. Almost all physiological proteins are also negatively charged, so that "like repelling like", an electrostatic barrier tends to prevent protein loss[1].

### Detection of Proteinuria

Normal urine contains protein composed of approximately 40% albumin, 20% other plasma proteins filtered at the glomerulus and 40% Tamm-Horsfall mucoproteins from tubular secretion. It is considered abnormal for an adult to excrete more than 150mg protein/24 hours[2].

The "gold standard" in detection of proteinuria remains the laboratory evaluation of 24-hour excretion, using the sulphosalicylic acid (Exton) test. This detects the presence of all proteins, but is clearly an inappropriate method for screening purposes.

### Screening for Proteinuria

In any form of screening, it is vital that patients with disease are not missed (false negatives), and unnecessary investigation is avoided (false positives).

The majority of side-room screening of urines is now performed using reagent strip tests, although some workers favour the use of protein/creatinine ratio as an index of proteinuria[3].

Is it valid to use a reagent strip for screening?

*Reagent strips measure the concentration of protein in a single specimen*

Reagent strips detect albumin in the main, being relatively insensitive to other proteins, e.g. Bence-Jones proteins. False positive and negative strip tests do occur (*Table 1*), for example if the urine is too concentrated or diluted. One of a family of reagent strips, N-MULTISTIX*SG tries to improve on the strip performance by including the specific gravity (SG). If the SG is less than 1.010 or is 1.030, caution is required in evaluating "Trace" proteinuria, with repeat testing recommended on more normal SG urine.

| Table 1 | |
| --- | --- |
| **Causes of False Negative and False Positive Protein Strip Tests** | |
| False positive strip test | Highly concentrated urine (SG≥1.030) |
| | Gross haematuria (macroscopic not microscopic) |
| | Highly alkaline urine (pH ≥8.0) |
| False negative strip test | Very dilute urine (SG ≤1.010) |
| | Tubular overload proteinuria (e.g. myeloma light chains) |

Random urine samples can be used to evaluate proteinuria

Reagent strips, it must be remembered, measure the *concentration* of protein in the single specimen tested, whereas proteinuria is defined in terms of 24-hour excretion. However, a good correlation exists between the concentration of protein in a "spot" sample and 24-hour total protein excretion (*Figure 1*), so that random samples can be used to evaluate proteinuria.

The N-MULTISTIX SG reagent strip was recently studied to determine its utility as a screening tool[4]. *Figure 2* shows a plot of 600 urinary reagent strip protein values against the total protein value for that specimen. There is clearly poor discrimination between "negative" and "trace" readings in relation to the corresponding laboratory values, but relatively high discrimination around the "trace or less/+ or more" boundary.

A false negative strip in isolated proteinuria is only of minor concern

Using only NEGATIVE/POSITIVE as the deciders, we achieved a specificity of 96%, and a sensitivity of 88%. However, of all the patients with false negative results, none excreted more than 900mg/24 hours. In the case of pure isolated proteinuria, none, therefore, would have fallen into a poor prognostic category. A false negative strip in isolated proteinuria is therefore only of minor concern.

"Trace" results could be further refined by repeat testing

"Trace" results could be further refined by the simple expedient of repeat testing through the day. If all strips show "trace" or less, 90% of patients will have normal protein excretion. If any strip shows "+" or more, then abnormal protein excretion may be expected in 82%.

Does the time of day when the sample is taken for testing influence the detection rate? Within our series, statistical analysis revealed no difference between samples, whether tested early in the morning, mid-morning or mid-afternoon. However, on an individual patient basis, 14/100 showed an orthostatic picture. Ten of these had associated haematuria, and would not therefore have slipped the investigative net[5]. Of the remainder, only three had no renal lesion and could truly be called orthostatic proteinurics. It is recommended therefore that screening of an ambulant specimen of urine, probably mid-morning, is most appropriate.

An ambulant mid-morning urine specimen is most appropriate

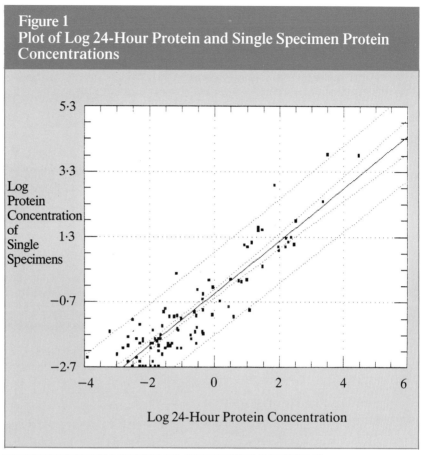

**Figure 1**
**Plot of Log 24-Hour Protein and Single Specimen Protein Concentrations**

Log Protein Concentration of Single Specimens

Log 24-Hour Protein Concentration

## INTERPRETATION OF THE N-MULTISTIX SG RESULTS

a)   Negative reagent strip   = Negative urine

b)   "+" or greater           = Positive urine

c)   "Trace" results refined by testing three samples:

       1)   "Trace" only        = Negative urine

       2)   "Trace"/Negative    = Negative urine

       3)   "Trace"/Positive    = Positive urine

All patients with positive urines warrant a 24-hour urine protein estimation.

*All patients with strip-positive urines warrant a 24-hour protein estimation*

## PROTEINURIA: CAUSES AND PATTERNS[2,6]

The causes of proteinuria are listed in *Figure 3*.

### Glomerular proteinuria

This may be selective (consisting almost entirely of albumin, the other filtered proteins being absorbed by the tubules), or unselective (consisting of a greater proportion of larger molecular weight proteins). This categorisation may be useful prognostically, especially in children with nephrotic syndrome.

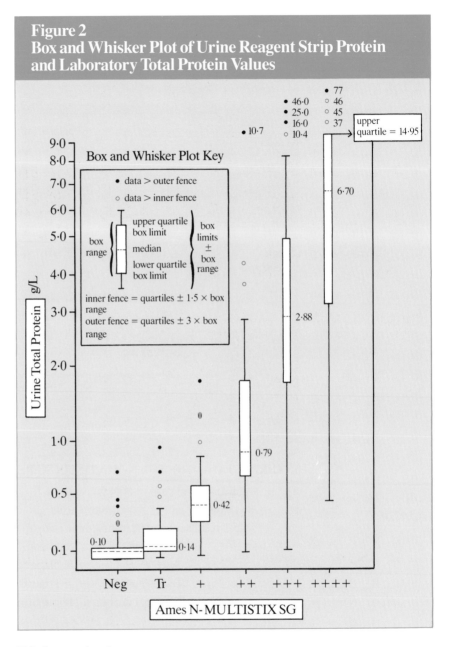

**Figure 2**
**Box and Whisker Plot of Urine Reagent Strip Protein and Laboratory Total Protein Values**

**Tubular proteinuria**

Tubular proteinuria may be seen in patients with normal glomeruli, occurring when either tubular damage prevents the reabsorption of filtered low molecular weight proteins, or with overload of the nephron by filtered proteins. Electrophoresis of urine reveals a predominance of alpha- and beta-globulins, with low levels of albumin. Usually there is less than 2g of proteinuria/24 hours.

## Figure 3
## Causes and Types of Proteinuria

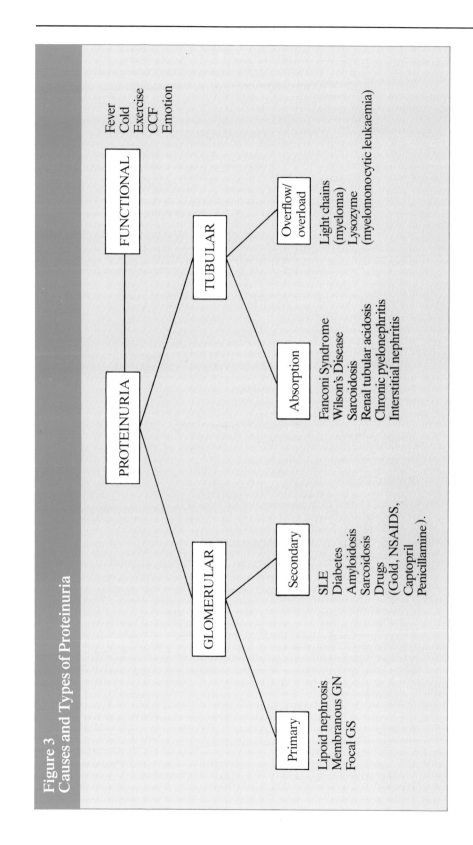

35

### Functional proteinuria

This occurs as a transient phenomenon during fever, severe exercise, emotional stress, exposure to cold, hypertension and congestive cardiac failure. It always disappears after resolution of the precipitating cause, and can be considered benign.

### ISOLATED PROTEINURIA

Isolated proteinuria is defined as proteinuria in the absence of any abnormal urinary sediment, or evidence of clinical abnormality, e.g. renal impairment, hypertension or significant structural abnormality. Its prognostic significance depends in part on the pattern of excretion determined during investigation, and on the degree of proteinuria (*Table 2*).

| Table 2 Recommended Follow-up Evaluation in Isolated Proteinuria | | | |
|---|---|---|---|
| **Pattern of Protein Excretion** | **Risk of ESRF** | **Recommended Evaluation** | **Follow-up Interval** |
| Transient | None | None | – |
| Intermittent (<150mg/24 hrs) | None | None | – |
| Intermittent (>150mg/24 hrs) | Slight | BP, urinalysis | Annual |
| Orthostatic | Slight | BP, urinalysis | 1–2 yrs |
| Constant | 20% after 10 yrs | BP, urinalysis Urea, creatinine | 6 monthly |

KEY: BP = Blood pressure.     ESRF = End-stage renal failure.

### Transient proteinuria

This is a very occasional finding in children and young adults, and disappears on repeat testing. This proteinuria is often "Functional", and never exceeds 150mg/day (140mg/24 hours/$m^2$ in children). It may recur occasionally, and is benign.

### Intermittent proteinuria

*Proteinuria is associated with an increased mortality in people over thirty, rising with age*

Proteinuria is present in approximately 50% of random urine samples. It usually occurs in young people under thirty years, and in this group it is not associated with an increase in mortality from renal disease. However, when found in an older age group, it is associated with an increased mortality which rises with increasing age. Up to 70% may have minor abnormalities on renal biopsy (e.g. mild mesangial proliferation). The majority lose their proteinuria over 5–10 years follow-up.

### Orthostatic proteinuria

Defined as proteinuria (>150mg/24 hours) which is present whilst in the upright posture, and disappearing after a period in the supine posture. During the period of rest – supine (usually overnight) – less than 50mg of protein is excreted. In young people with proteinuria, this pattern is present in 15%. In general it can be considered benign and in the majority, renal biopsy findings are normal. However, it can be found as a feature of resolving glomerulonephritis or pyelonephritis. Most lose their proteinuria, but in those in whom it persists the prognosis is good even after 20 years follow-up. A small minority develop constant proteinuria with its worst prognosis.

### Constant proteinuria

Hypertension develops in 50% of patients with constant proteinuria over five years. End-stage renal failure develops in 20% over ten years

Constant proteinuria is a cause for concern. Its prognosis is as heterogeneous as its aetiology. Renal biopsy reveals a wide variety of abnormalities, from mild mesangial proliferation with its better prognosis, to abnormalities with the potential or the development of end-stage renal failure (ESRF), e.g. focal segmental glomerulonephritis (GN), membranous GN, focal glomerulosclerosis, and membrano-proliferative GN. Hypertension develops in 50% of patients over five years, and end stage renal failure in 20% over ten years follow-up.

### INVESTIGATION OF PROTEINURIA

See *Figure 4.*

The majority of patients with abnormal proteinuria will have glomerular disease

The majority of patients with abnormal proteinuria will have glomerular disease, and thus the finding of abnormal proteinuria should prompt further investigation.

The presence of haematuria with proteinuria is always abnormal, and almost always warrants renal biopsy

Investigations are performed to clarify the underlying lesion and assist in treatment and prognosis. The presence of haematuria with proteinuria is always abnormal, and almost always warrants renal biopsy[5]. In general, in isolated proteinuria, the excretion of less than 2G/24 hours of protein (an arbitrary cut-off) is associated with a good prognosis[6], and requires only to be kept under surveillance. More than 2G/24 hours requires renal biopsy to further categorise the renal lesion.

### References

1. Cameron, J.S. "Proteinuria and the Nephrotic Syndrome," in Oxford Textbook of Medicine. (1984); Chapter 18, 52.

2. Abuelo, J.G. Proteinuria: Diagnostic principles and procedures. Annals of Internal Medicine (1983); **98**: 186–191.

3. Shaw, A.B., Risdon, P., Lewis-Jackson, J.D. Protein creatinine index and Albustix in assessment of proteinuria. Brit.Med.J. (1983); **287**: 929–932.

4. Harrison, N.A., Rainford, D.J., Cullen, S.A., White, G.A., Strike, P.W. Proteinuria – What value is the dipstick? Brit.J.Urol. (1989); **63**: 202–208.

5. Arm, J.P., Peile, E.B., Rainford, D.J., Significance of dipstick haematuria. 2. Correlation with pathology. Brit.J.Urol. (1986); **58**: 218–223.

6. Stewart, D.W., Gordon, J.A., Schoolwerth, A.C. Evaluation of proteinuria. Am.Fam.Physician (1984); **29**: 218–225.

## Figure 4
## Algorithm for the Investigation of Proteinuria

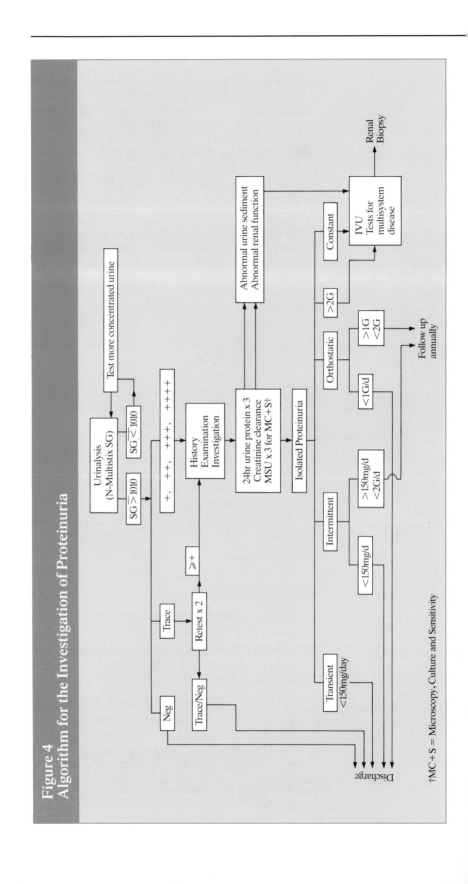

†MC + S = Microscopy, Culture and Sensitivity

# Microalbuminuria in the Diagnosis and Prevention of Diabetic Renal Disease

**Dr. G. F. Watts**

Lecturer, Department of Endocrinology and Chemical Pathology, UMDS, St. Thomas' Hospital, London

### Introduction

Nephropathy is the major cause of morbidity and mortality in young insulin-dependent diabetic patients (IDDs). Classical diabetic nephropathy is characterised by persistent clinical proteinuria (ALBUSTIX* positive; urinary protein >0.5g/24hr), elevated serum creatinine, arterial hypertension, advanced retinopathy and long duration of diabetes. Clinical proteinuria heralds a unique and inexorable decline in renal function to end-stage uraemia; it also substantially accelerates the rate of macrovascular disease. Because the treatment of established diabetic nephropathy is generally unsatisfactory, many patients eventually require renal replacement therapy, the health and socio-economic burdens of which are immense. A major precedent has, therefore, been established for earlier diagnosis and prevention of diabetic renal disease.

*Clinical proteinuria heralds the decline to end-stage renal failure, and accelerates macrovascular disease*

### Early Diabetic Renal Involvement

Several functional and morphological abnormalities have been described in the diabetic kidney prior to the onset of clinical proteinuria (*Table 1*).

---

**Table 1**
**Early Renal Changes in Diabetes Mellitus**

- ↑ Albumin Excretion
- ↑ Glomerular Filtration Rate
- ↑ Renal Blood Flow
- ↑ Filtration Fraction
- ↑ Renal Size
- ↑ Glomerular Basement Membrane (GBM)
- ↑ Mesangial Expansion
- ↓ GBM Anionic Charge
- ↓ GBM Proteoglycan Turnover

---

Although hyperfiltration (elevation of the glomerular filtration rate, renal blood flow and filtration fraction) and ultrastructural changes (glomerular basement membrane thickening and mesangial expansion) are early features of diabetic renal disease, the most clinically relevant abnormality is a raised excretion of urinary albumin – referred to as "sub-clinical albuminuria" or "microalbuminuria".

## MICROALBUMINURIA

### 1. Definition

The term microalbuminuria was first used by Keen et al (1969) and later emphasised by Viberti et al (1982). Microalbuminuria is conventionally defined as a quantity of urinary albumin excretion (timed collection) above the reference range for healthy non-diabetic subjects, but which escapes detection by indicator dye-binding methods such as ALBUSTIX (ALBUSTIX reagent strip "1+" corresponds to 200–300 mg/L of urinary albumin).

Although there is a good correlation between various methods of urine collection, the commonly employed ones have been 24-hour (Danish studies) and overnight samples (Guy's Hospital studies). The range of urinary albumin excretion in normal adults is 2–26mg/24 hr and 1–9μg/min in overnight collections. Abnormal urinary albumin excretion may also be defined in terms of an albumin concentration and an albumin:creatinine ratio. *Table 2* gives adult reference ranges for various expressions of urinary albumin excretion likely to be used when screening for and monitoring microalbuminuria.

## Table 2
## Overnight, Recumbent (OR) and Daytime, Ambulant (DA) Urinary Albumin Excretion in Healthy Adult Subjects (n=127)

| Urine Collection | Albumin Excretion Measurement | Geometric mean | 95% range |
|:---:|:---:|:---:|:---:|
| OR | $U_A$ | 3.9[a] | 0.9–16.2 |
| OR | $U_A/U_C$ | 0.4[c] | 0.1– 1.0 |
| OR | $U_AV$ | 3.2[e] | 1.2– 8.6 |
| DA | $U_A$ | 5.1[b] | 0.9–29.6 |
| DA | $U_A/U_C$ | 0.6[d] | 0.1– 2.3 |
| DA | $U_AV$ | 4.5[f] | 1.0–19.1 |

Albumin concentration ($U_A$, mg/L); albumin/creatinine ratio ($U_A/U_C$, mg/mmol); albumin excretion rate ($U_AV$, μg/min).

[a]vs [b], $p < 0.001$; [c] vs [d], $p < 0.001$; [e] vs [f], $p < 0.001$.

Microalbuminuria may also be defined with reference to thresholds of albumin excretion above which the risk of future nephropathy is substantially increased (*Table 3*). Repeated measurements will identify intermittent, persistent and progressive patterns of microalbuminuria. The use of ALBUSTIX in the *definition* of microalbuminuria is not strictly recommended, as the reagent strip detects other urinary proteins besides albumin and may also misclassify very concentrated and dilute urines; the "ceiling value" for microalbuminuria should be between 200–300μg/minute.

### 2. Pathogenesis

The most attractive hypothesis suggests that microalbuminuria is due to loss of the charge-restrictive properties of the glomerular barrier. As microalbuminuria increases, the selectivity of the microproteinuria falls. This implies an increased filtration of polyanionic albumin molecules relative to neutral IgG molecules, resulting from loss of the fixed negative electrical charge of the glomerular membrane. Depletion of the glycosaminoglycan content may account for reduction in anionic membrane charge; genetic polymorphism of enzymes

As microalbuminuria increases, the selectivity of the microproteinuria falls involved in the metabolism of heparan sulphate proteoglycan (e.g. N-deacetylase) may explain the variation in the susceptibility of individual patients to microalbuminuria and diabetic nephropathy. Poor glycaemic control may be critical not only in reducing glycosaminoglycan turnover, but also in preferentially increasing the filtration of glycosylated albumin. The accumulation of albumin and other macromolecules in the glomerular mesangium is thought to initiate the structural and haemodynamic changes that lead to overt nephropathy. It has recently been proposed that a genetic predisposition to hypertension may be linked to the development of microalbuminuria. There is some evidence that microalbuminuria may have a renal tubular component.

## 3. Prognostic Significance and Natural History

Four prospective studies have shown that microalbuminuria is a powerful predictor of clinical nephropathy in IDD's (*Table 3*).

### Table 3
### Levels of Urinary Albumin Excretion Predictive (>75%) of Overt Nephropathy or Premature Cardiovascular Mortality in Diabetes Mellitus

| Study | Type of Diabetes | Threshold Albumin Excretion Rate ($\mu$g/min) | Urine Collection | Follow-up (years) |
|---|---|---|---|---|
| Steno Memorial Hospital (1982) | IDDM | 28 | 24 hr | 6 |
| Guy's Hospital (1982) | IDDM | 30 | Overnight | 14 |
| Steno Memorial Hospital (1984) | IDDM | 70 | 24 hr | 6 |
| Aarhus University (1984) | IDDM | 15 | Daytime, resting | 10 |
| Guy's Hospital (1984) | NIDDM | 10 | Overnight | 14 |
| Aarhus University (1984) | NIDDM | 15† | Early morning | 10 |

†mg/L

The variation in the thresholds of albumin excretion among the studies is due to differences in the clinical features of the cohorts of patients, the methods of urine sampling and the length of follow-up.

Microalbuminuria is an independent concomitant of CHD in NIDDs and is a powerful predictor of nephropathy in IDDs

Microalbuminuria also predicts clinical proteinuria and cardiovascular mortality in NIDD's. Preliminary evidence suggests that the emergence of microalbuminuria in diabetic pregnancy adversely affects the foetus, but further work is required.

Patients with persistent microalbuminuria ("incipient nephropathy") or albumin excretion greater than 70μg/minute, especially if associated with hyperfiltration, have the worst prognosis. Mogensen et al (1985) have suggested that the albumin excretion rate increases by about 20% per year in the phase of "incipient nephropathy". Progression of microalbuminuria appears to be most consistently related to the prevailing systemic blood pressure. The mean annual rate of progression from normoalbuminuria to microalbuminuria is as slow as 0.7%. The annual incidence of persistent microalbuminuria in patients with initially normal albumin excretion is about 2% for IDDs and 3% for NIDDs.

### 4. Prevalence and Associations

The prevalence of microalbuminuria in diabetic outpatients ranges between 6 and 40%, depending on the threshold level of albumin excretion, the method of urine sampling and the clinical characteristics of the patients. That microalbuminuria is commoner in non-insulin-dependent diabetic patients (NIDDs) of Asian-Indian extraction than in Europeans is consistent with their higher predisposition to diabetic nephropathy.

Several physiological and clinical factors are associated with raised albumin excretion (*Table 4*).

---

**Table 4**
**Factors Associated with Microalbuminuria**

- Early onset of diabetes
- Long duration of diabetes
- Systemic hypertension
- Family history of hypertension
- Retinopathy
- Neuropathy
- Hyperglycaemia
- Male sex
- Smoking
- ↓ Aerobic working capacity
- ↑ Myocardial contractility
- ↑ Low density lipoprotein/high density lipoprotein ratio
- ↑ Transcapillary escape rate of albumin
- ↑ Von Willebrand Factor
- ↑ Erythrocyte sodium-lithium countertransport

---

Albumin excretion is higher when upright and ambulant than when recumbent. Moderate exercise can induce microalbuminuria in diabetics, but not in control subjects. A transient elevation in albumin excretion rate may arise from an acute increase in the urine flow, e.g. after a water load, but not during steady diuresis.

The larger studies in IDDs have consistently related microalbuminuria to early onset of diabetes, arterial hypertension, proliferative retinopathy and peripheral neuropathy. Male sex, pregnancy, smoking, long duration of diabetes, poor glycaemic control and increased dietary protein and fat may also be important associations. A family history of hypertension and raised erythrocyte sodium-lithium counter-transport have recently been linked to microalbuminuria and clinical nephropathy in IDDs.

Lipoprotein disturbances, increased vascular permeability to macromolecules, and haemorheological changes in IDDs with persistent microalbuminuria may increase their risk of premature atherosclerosis; echocardiographic studies have also revealed pronounced cardiac hyperfunction consistent with a state of tissue hyperperfusion. Microalbuminuria is an independent concomitant of coronary heart disease in NIDDs.

Since the clinical associations are only modest, a selective screening protocol for microalbuminuria cannot at present be recommended. However, where costing and manpower are important, it will be helpful to focus the measurement of albumin excretion on patients with early onset of diabetes, proliferative retinopathy, absent ankle reflexes, elevated blood pressure (compared to controls matched for age and sex), family history of hypertension and raised glycated haemoglobin. Diabetic children with poor long-term glycaemic control are a group of patients that merits special attention. Although hyperfiltration may increase the risk of clinical nephropathy in patients with microalbuminuria, the methodologies for accurately estimating the glomerular filtration rate (GFR) are at present too impracticable for routine use.

In interpreting an abnormal level of albumin excretion, attention should be paid to "false positives" arising from undue exertion, high fever, emotional stress, cold exposure, acute water intake, contamination of urine by menstrual flow or semen, and urinary tract infection especially if associated with haematuria (*Table 5*).

## Table 5
## Potential Sources of "False-Positives" when Screening for Microalbuminuria in Diabetes Mellitus

- Exercise
- Acute fluid intake
- Haematuria
- Menstrual flow
- Urinary infection
- Renal papillary necrosis
- Semen
- Urine collection error
- Laboratory error

Urinary infection and haematuria may be rapidly detected in the clinic by N-MULTISTIX* SG. Congestive cardiac failure, essential hypertension and non-diabetic renal disease may also induce microalbuminuria.

### 5. Measurement

### a) Immunoassays

Immunochemical assays meet the requirements of sensitivity (urinary albumin concentration less than 5mg/L), specificity and reliability for the estimation of low concentration urinary albumin excretion corresponding to microalbuminuria;

precision and accuracy are essential when monitoring the course of microalbuminuria. For very dilute urines, highly sensitive assays such as enzyme-linked immunoassay (EIA) and radioimmunoassay (RIA) are required. Practicability and cost are important considerations, but the choice of assay is likely to depend on the local technical expertise and instrumentation. Although several commercial kits are available, "in-house" methodologies are considerably cheaper. Use of centrifugal analysers such as the Cobas-Fara (Roche Diagnostics) has specific merits related to speed of analysis and simultaneous measurement of other pertinent analytes such as fructosamine, creatinine and lipids. There is an existing demand for standardisation of methods and quality assurance schemes. Urine samples for immunoassays may be stored at $-20°C$ with sodium azide as preservative for up to six months; there is disagreement regarding the need to avoid centrifugation of samples and adjustment of urinary pH to 7.0 prior to assay.

### b) Side-Room Tests

In large-scale screening programmes for microalbuminuria, laboratory and clinical workload will be relieved by the use of simple side-room tests. Although technically unskilled personnel working in hospital out-patient or GP clinics may carry out these tests, some training will be required. The tests are based on turbidimetry, the "protein error of indicators" principle, or latex immunoagglutination (*Figure 1*); they can be made sensitive down to a urinary albumin concentration of 15–30mg/litre and are best used qualitatively.

An immunoagglutination test is most desirable because of its specificity for albumin. "Prozone inhibition" i.e. inhibition of agglutination at high albumin concentrations, is a drawback of some immunoagglutination methods, but may be detected by simultaneously testing the urine with ALBUSTIX. Alternatively, the recently developed Albusure (Cambridge Life Sciences) protects against "Prozone Inhibition".

*MICRO-BUMINTEST is probably the most practicable of the side-room tests*

Indicator dye-binding tests such as MICRO-BUMINTEST* (Ames) are probably the most practicable of the side-room tests.

A comparison of the three principal types of tests is summarised in *Tables 6 and 7*.

These were performed on early morning urine samples from 100 insulin-dependent diabetic patients attending a hospital diabetic clinic. A prototype (MICRO-ALBUTEST*) of MICRO-BUMINTEST was used for this study. The sulphosalicylic acid test and MICRO-BUMINTEST, being non-immunological, will also detect proteins other than albumin. This may have clinical significance. For example, increased IgGuria may be the first indication of loss of the size-restrictive properties of the glomerular filtration barrier. Further studies are required.

*The detection of proteins other than albumin may have clinical significance*

Since some side-room tests only measure albumin concentration, they may fail to detect patients with low level albuminuria in very dilute urines. Dilute urine in a diabetic patient may be due to poor metabolic control, which may be conveniently assessed in the clinic by testing the urine for glycosuria with N-LABSTIX*. Potential "false negatives" should be screened in the laboratory using the albumin:creatinine ratio (see *Figure 2*).

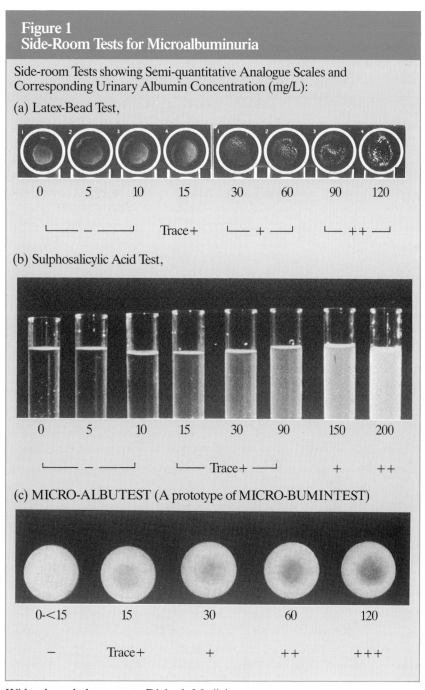

# Figure 1
## Side-Room Tests for Microalbuminuria

Side-room Tests showing Semi-quantitative Analogue Scales and Corresponding Urinary Albumin Concentration (mg/L):

(a) Latex-Bead Test,

| 0 | 5 | 10 | 15 | 30 | 60 | 90 | 120 |

|—— − ——| Trace+ |— + —| |— ++ —|

(b) Sulphosalicylic Acid Test,

| 0 | 5 | 10 | 15 | 30 | 90 | 150 | 200 |

|—— − ——| |—— Trace+ ——| + ++

(c) MICRO-ALBUTEST (A prototype of MICRO-BUMINTEST)

| 0-<15 | 15 | 30 | 60 | 120 |

− Trace+ + ++ +++

With acknowledgements to Diabetic Medicine.

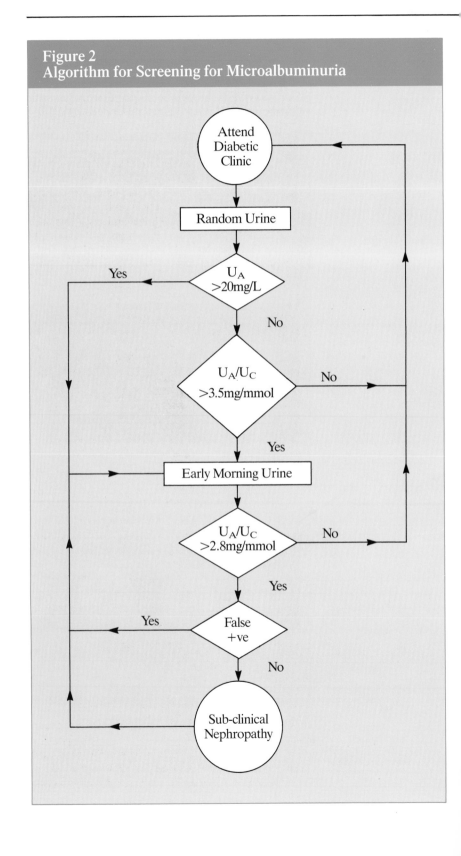

## Table 6
## Comparison of Practicability of Latex Bead Immunoagglutination Test, Sulphosalicylic Acid Test and MICRO-BUMINTEST

|  | LBT | SST | MBT |
|---|---|---|---|
| Sample Volume ($\mu$l) | 25 | 1000 | 25 |
| Number of Reagent Additions | 2 | 1 | 1 |
| Reagent Shelf-Life (Days) | <4 | >365 | 3 years |
| Need for Centrifugation or Filtration | No | Yes | No |
| Technical Skill Required | Most | Middle | Least |
| Hours for 100 Tests | 1.5 | 0.5 | 0.75 |

LBT = Latex Bead Immunoagglutination
SST = Sulphosalicylic Acid
MBT = MICRO-BUMINTEST

## Table 7
## Performance and Screening Validity (RIA Albumin Concentrations Above 30 mg/L) of Side-Room Tests

|  | LBT | SST | MBT |
|---|---|---|---|
| Reproducibility by 2 Operators[x](%) | 100 | 100 | 100 |
| Concordance of 9 Standards by 10 Observers[†] (%) | 100 | 100 | 100 |
| Sensitivity (%) | 100 | 100 | 100 |
| Specificity (%) | 88 | 86 | 91 |
| Positive Predictive Value (%) | 64 | 67 | 72 |
| Negative Predictive Value (%) | 97 | 96 | 100 |

[x] Skilled
[†] Unskilled
LBT = Latex Bead Immunoagglutination
SST = Sulphosalicylic Acid Test
MBT = MICRO-BUMINTEST

### c) Methods of Urine Collection for Screening and Monitoring

There is a good correlation between the various methods of urine collection for albumin excretion, whether timed or untimed. The most practicable should be used to screen for microalbuminuria and the most accurate (least within-subject variation) to monitor the subsequent pattern and its response to treatment. Since timed urine collections (particularly over 24 hours) are notoriously inaccurate and cumbersome for patients and laboratories, non-timed samples provide the most convenient tests. The accuracy of the urinary albumin concentration alone is increased by estimating the albumin to creatinine ratio in the same sample; this ratio may need to be corrected for body size when studying children, and account may occasionally have to be taken of the consumption of cooked meats (e.g. roast beef) that significantly increase creatinine excretion. Although a random clinic sample may be used as a primary screening test, the lower within-subject variability of recumbent than ambulant albumin excretion suggests that resting samples, e.g. the early morning albumin to creatinine ratio, should be used to accurately assess whether a patient has intermittent, persistent or progressive microalbuminuria.

### d) Screening Protocol for Microalbuminuria

An algorithm based on non-timed urine collections for screening for microalbuminuria ($U_AV>30\mu g/min$) is given in *Figure 2*.

Side-room tests detect urinary albumin concentration and can therefore be incorporated into this protocol. In children and in adults with albumin excretion close to the upper limit of normal, the urinary albumin:creatinine ratio ($U_A/U_C$) will need to be corrected for body size. Retesting, which may be required over several years, should be more frequent in patients with a greater degree of microalbuminuria and the following clinical features: age at onset of diabetes less than ten years; duration of diabetes between 10 and 20 years; advanced retinopathy; poor long-term glycaemic control; clinical hypertension.
As indicated by these criteria, the interval between tests will vary between 2 and 18 months.

### Urinary Excretion of Other Proteins

Although increased urinary excretion of low molecular weight proteins (e.g. retinol-binding protein), intermediate molecular weight proteins (e.g. transferrin) and tubular wall enzymes (e.g. N-acetyl-ß-D-glucosaminidase) have been described in diabetic patients without clinical nephropathy, the prognostic significance of these findings is unknown. However, the urinary excretion of large molecular weight proteins (e.g. IgG) may serve to characterise the selectivity of microproteinuria and hence the extent of glomerular damage.

### 6. Therapy

The following conclusions are based on recently-published clinical trials involving small numbers of IDDs and carried out over periods of between one and five years.

Tight glycaemic control and lowering blood pressure may retard or reverse the progression of microalbuminuria

Tight glycaemic control using continuous subcutaneous insulin infusion retards or reverses the progression of microalbuminuria: the best outcome may be achieved by treating albumin excretion just above the reference range. Control of hypertension with cardioselective beta blockers and diuretics reduces microalbuminuria. Angiotension Converting Enzyme (ACE) inhibitors (e.g. Enalapril, Captopril), which lower both intra-glomerular and systemic blood pressures, prevent the development of clinical nephropathy in normotensive patients with persistent microalbuminuria; they can also eliminate microalbuminuria induced by exercise. By contrast, calcium-channel blockers (e.g. Adalat) may aggravate microalbuminuria in certain patients. Although some benefit may accrue from reduction in dietary protein intake (c40g/day), and specific inhibition of thromboxane synthetase and aldose reductase, further clinical trials are required.

In spite of these encouraging reports, there is no existing evidence that end-stage renal failure or mortality is modified by the above treatments. The results of large-scale clinical trials currently being conducted in the USA (Diabetic Control and Complications Trial) and in the UK (Microalbuminuria Collaborative Study) are keenly awaited.

Meanwhile it seems prudent to optimise glycaemic and arterial blood pressure control in all patients with microalbuminuria. It should be noted that blood pressure may need to be lowered within the reference range matched for age and sex.

Preliminary studies in NIDDs have confirmed the benefits of improved metabolic and blood pressure control.

## CONCLUSIONS

The measurement of microalbuminuria allows early detection of insulin-dependent diabetic patients at risk of developing overt nephropathy. Impressive evidence suggests that microalbuminuria and the subsequent course to irreversible nephropathy may be beneficially influenced by lowering blood pressure and optimising glycaemic control.

While definitive evidence is awaited that the course to end-stage renal failure is averted by these and other therapies, the measurement of microalbuminuria should be an integral part of the assessment and monitoring of insulin-dependent diabetes mellitus and its complications. This recommendation also applies to non-insulin dependent diabetic patients, since they form a significant proportion of the diabetic renal failure population and are also particularly at risk of macrovascular disease.

### Further Reading

Deckert, T., Feldt-Rasmussen, B., Borch-Johnsen, K., Jensen, T., Kofoed-Enevoldsen, A. Albuminuria reflects widespread vascular damage: The Steno Hypothesis. Diabetologia (1989); **32**: 219–226.

Mogensen, C.E., Schmitz, A., Christensen, C.K. Comparative renal pathophysiology relevant to IDDM and NIDDM patients. Diabetes and Metabolism Reviews (1988); **4**: 453–483.

Mogensen, C.E. Microalbuminuria as a predictor of clinical diabetic nephropathy. Kidney International (1987); **31**: 673–689.

Rosenstock, J., Raskin, P. Early diabetic nephropathy: assessment and potential therapeutic interventions. Diabetes Care (1986); **9**: 529–545.

Viberti, G.C., Keen, H. The patterns of proteinuria in diabetes mellitus. Diabetes (1984); **33**: 686–692.

Viberti, G.C., Wiseman, M.J. The Kidney in diabetes: Significance of the early abnormalities. Clinics in Endocrinology and Metabolism (1986); **15**: 783–806.

Watts, G.F., Hodgson, B., Morris, R.W., Shaw, K.M., Polak, A. Side-room tests to screen for microalbuminuria in diabetes mellitus. Diabetic Medicine (1988); **5**: 298–303.

Watts, G.F., Bennett, J.E., Rowe, D.J., Morris, R.W., Gatling, W., Shaw, K.M., Polak, A. Assessment of immunochemical methods for determining low concentrations of albumin in urine. Clinical Chemistry (1986); **32(8)**: 1544–1548.

# Urinary Tract Infection: An Overview

**Professor M. Sussman**
Department of Microbiology, Medical School,
Newcastle upon Tyne

Urinary tract infection (UTI) may be defined as the presence of an infectious agent in any part of the urinary tract, excluding the urethra. By far the commonest agents responsible for UTI are bacteria, and this account will be confined to bacterial UTI.

It is necessary to distinguish between asymptomatic UTI, conventionally termed *covert bacteriuria* (CBU), and symptomatic UTI. The latter may remain essentially limited to the bladder (cystitis), or it may ascend the urinary tract to involve the kidney (acute pyelonephritis, APN). Under certain circumstances, UTI can lead to permanent and progressive structural damage of the renal parenchyma (chronic pyelonephritis, CPN).

*Urine is likely to become contaminated while it is being passed*

Since urine is likely to become contaminated while it is being passed, its collection and examination for the diagnosis for UTI must be subject to special criteria.

*It is important to distinguish between infection and contamination*

These criteria are based on quantitative bacteriology, by means of which it is possible to distinguish reliably between accidental contamination of the collected urine and true infection, i.e. the presence of bacteria within the urinary tract. This distinction has made it possible to study the natural history and epidemiology of UTI, and to define the factors that constitute a risk of lower UTI progressing to acute pyelonephritis or chronic pyelonephritis.

## 1. THE CONCEPT OF SIGNIFICANT BACTERIURIA

As we have already noted, a basic necessity in urine bacteriology is to distinguish between specimens that show infection and those that are merely contaminated. It has been shown by Kass[1] and others that, provided urine is collected with care to avoid contamination, a count of $\geq 10^5$ colony forming units (cfu) of bacteria/ml of urine indicates infection of the urinary tract with a probability of >80%. A second specimen with a similar count brings the probability to between 90 and 100%. Such a finding is termed *significant bacteriuria*. As first described, it referred to females who were asymptomatic and from whom first-morning specimens of urine had been collected. The relationship between bacterial count and the probability of the presence of infection is shown in *Figure 1*.

This is the basis of quantitative bacteriology in the diagnosis of UTI. Several points must, however, be emphasised. The presence of more than one type of organism is suggestive of contamination rather than infection, except in chronic infections, or in the presence of abnormalities of the urinary tract, or other complicating features including the presence of a catheter or other instrumentation. Specimens of urine, other than first-morning specimens, collected from patients with acute UTI may show lower counts than $10^5$ cfu/ml. This may be due to frequency and the increased fluid intake which patients may find alleviates their dysuria. In any case, significant bacteriuria is merely a laboratory finding, and other clinical factors must always be taken into account.

*Up to 40% of specimens received in the laboratory are urines. 60% to 80% of these show no evidence of infection*

## 2. DETECTION OF UTI

Traditionally, examination of urine for infection consists of labour-intensive microscopy followed by cultural procedures. However, since up to 40% of

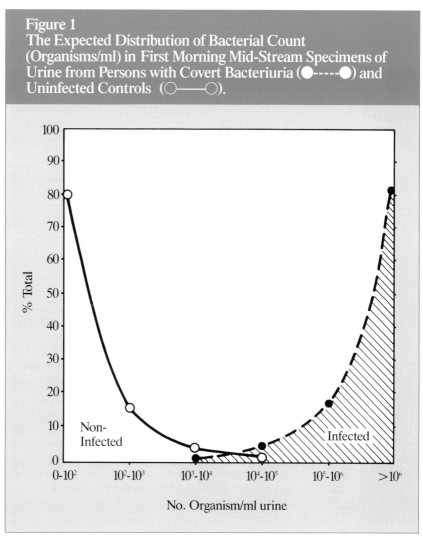

**Figure 1**
The Expected Distribution of Bacterial Count (Organisms/ml) in First Morning Mid-Stream Specimens of Urine from Persons with Covert Bacteriuria (●-----●) and Uninfected Controls (○——○).

Reproduced by permission of Blackwell Scientific Publications Limited

specimens received in the average clinical microbiology laboratory are urines and 60% to 80% of these show no evidence of infection, the use of simple and rapid screening procedures is desirable and indeed, in these times of financial stringency, is fully justified.

### 2.1 Collection of Urine

The quality of the results obtained from examination of the urine can only be as good as the quality of the specimen provided. The technique of specimen collection is therefore crucial.

The normal urinary tract is sterile, apart from the greater part of the female urethra and the terminal urethra in the male. Thus, normal urine would be sterile were it not that it is likely to become contaminated while it is being

The quality of results can only be as good as the quality of the specimen collected. To reduce this risk, urine is most commonly collected as a midstream urine (MSU), the assumption being that potential contaminants are washed out of the urethra by the initial part of the stream. In males this is a reasonable assumption, and satisfactory specimens can be collected with a modicum of co-operation, provided that the foreskin is retracted. In women, collection of uncontaminated specimens requires far greater care and co-operation. The introitus should be cleaned with water or saline-soaked swabs; antiseptics must never be used. If it is thought necessary, "soft soap" (sapo mollis) may be used. The labia should be held apart and a MSU collected.

Antiseptics must never be used prior to urine collection

The collection of catheter specimens of urine (CSU) is to be deplored and cannot be justified unless there are other cogent clinical indications for catheterisation, which must always be carried out with due regard to the highest standards of asepsis. Even then, it should not be a cause for surprise if a proportion of patients develop a UTI as a result of catheterisation.

Catheterisation may induce a UTI

An uncommonly used but safe and reliable method for obtaining uncontaminated urine is suprapubic aspiration.

## 2.2 Examination of Urine

### i) Microscopy

Examination of urine conventionally begins with microscopy, by which means micro-organisms and cells can be seen. Uncentrifuged urine is examined as a "wet film" at lower power ($\times 40$) under standardised conditions, so that the volume of urine being observed in a single microscope field is known, or at least is reproducible, and this facilitates the counting of leucocytes. The presence of more than $10^4$ leucocytes/ml may indicate infection.

It has been shown that in the presence of significant bacteriuria with or without symptoms, there are usually more than $10^4$ leucocytes/ml of uncentrifuged urine. Nevertheless, pyuria is not a useful guide to the existence of infection. Its presence depends on the rate of urine production, and pyuria may persist for several days while infection is resolving. Pyuria in the presence of sterile urine should arouse suspicion of tuberculosis, neoplasia or even of a foreign body.

Pyuria in the presence of sterile urine should arouse suspicion of tuberculosis, neoplasia, or a foreign body

It is a useful rule of thumb that if, under these conditions of microscopy, bacteria are seen without the need for a search, it is probable that $>10^5$ organisms/ml are present.

### ii) Cultural Methods

Direct methods for the diagnosis of UTI are based on bacteriological culture. The available methods fall into the following three groups: semi-quantitative, quantitative and qualitative.

A variety of semi-quantitative cultural methods are available[2]. The best known and most commonly used is the dip-slide, the surfaces of which are coated with two media; one is selective and the other is non-selective. The former provides an estimate of the number of uropathogens, while the latter acts as a screen for contaminants. The dip-slide is dipped into the urine under test and, after incubation, any growth is compared with standard illustrations. The dip-slide can be used as a screen for bacteriuria in the community, or as the semi-quantitative part of the systematic investigation of urines in the clinical laboratory.

Strictly quantitative culture methods depend on the inoculation of appropriate media with measured volumes of accurately diluted urine, so that precise colony counts are obtained. Such methods are rarely used for routine purposes, but may be useful for research.

In the routine clinical laboratory, the usual approach is to obtain a semi-quantitative estimate of the colony count, and at the same time or subsequently to carry out a qualitative examination of the urine to isolate and identify the pathogens that may be present. It is always essential that urine is cultured on a non-selective medium, so that contaminated specimens can be identified and excluded.

## 3. THE CAUSATIVE ORGANISMS OF UTI

The commonest source of the organisms that cause UTI is the bowel, and the commonest urinary pathogen under all circumstances is *Escherichia coli*. However, other organisms may cause UTI in a small proportion of cases.

With community patients, more than 80% of acute UTI in individuals with structurally normal urinary tracts is due to *E. coli*. The remaining infections may be due to a variety of organisms. The distribution of causative organisms in hospital out-patients is somewhat different, but *E. coli* remains predominant. In hospital in-patients, in chronic UTI, or where the urinary tract is 'abnormal' (e.g. uncorrected congenital abnormalities, obstructive uropathy, etc.), a smaller proportion of UTI is due to *E. coli* (*Table 1*).

### Table 1
### Typical Distribution of Organisms Isolated from Patients with Urinary Tract Infection

|  | Covert Bacteriuria | UTI in In-Patients | UTI in Out-Patients |
|---|---|---|---|
| *Escherichia coli* | 84.1 | 47 | 64 |
| *Proteus mirabilis* | 8.4 | 21 | 15 |
| *Klebsiella aerogenes* | 1.9 | 7 | 4 |
| Other coliforms |  | 17 | 9 |
| Gram-positive spp | 0.9 | 8 | 8 |

In uncircumcised young boys, *Proteus* spp. are common urinary pathogens. Their origin is probably from the secretions in the prepucial sac, which tend to harbour these organisms.

The second most common urinary pathogen in young women between the ages of 15 and 35 is *Staphylococcus saprophyticus*. This appears to be related to sexual activity, but the nature of the relationship remains elusive.

The possible involvement of fastidious organisms and anaerobes in UTI is controversial, though it would be surprising if on occasion they were not involved, particularly in the presence of advanced or complicated disease. It should be remembered that such organisms are not likely to be observed when standard methods of culture are used. The possibility that tubercle bacilli may be responsible for upper UTI should not be neglected, especially in the presence of mixed infections and pyuria recalcitrant to conventional antimicrobial therapy.

*Candida albicans* is the commonest cause of fungal UTI. Such infection is usually related to broad spectrum antimicrobial therapy, immunosuppression, instrumentation, anatomical abnormality or foreign bodies.

## 4. SCREENING METHODS

For our purposes, screening may be defined as the application of simple and rapid procedures for sifting a group of specimens to find those that require detailed attention, so that the others can be discarded. It is clear that such procedures are potentially extremely valuable.

Healthy individuals excrete variable amounts of nitrate, and a chemical screening method for bacteriuria depends on the fact that bacteria reduce the nitrate to nitrite during growth. Screening tests are carried out with reagent strips, and positive tests demonstrate the presence of nitrite. For this test to be reliable, it is necessary that bacterial growth in the bladder has had sufficient time for the required change to take place. Usually, this is overnight, and the test is best done on an early-morning urine. Unfortunately, certain organisms such as *Enterococcus* and *Pseudomonas* do not reduce nitrate.

Since at least symptomatic UTI is accompanied by inflammation, protein, leucocytes and red cells may be present in the urine, and these can be tested for by means of reagent strips. The presence of proteinuria, i.e. the presence of protein in the urine in amounts greater than normal, is not of itself a useful indicator of infection. Excretion of up to about 150mg of protein/24 hours is usual, and certain physiological factors – such as orthostatic proteinuria – may more than double the rate of protein excretion. In addition, the reagent strips are highly sensitive to protein.

Leucocytes contain an esterase that can be detected by a reagent strip method on the basis of its ability to convert an ester substrate into a blue derivative (indigo) in the presence of air. The test has a sensitivity and a specificity of about 90%. Provided that it is not assumed that pyuria indicates bacteriuria, this is a useful test when carried out at the same time as other screening tests.

Haematuria is part of the inflammatory phenomena of acute UTI, and may thus be associated with bacteriuria and pyuria. It persists for some time after successful treatment, and is a feature of a wide variety of conditions including non-bacterial infections. Haematuria alone is, therefore, not a useful screening indicator for UTI.

The value of screening tests can be enhanced if tests are carried out in combination. Thus, it has been shown by Lowe[3] that, when the N-LABSTIX* reagent strip tests for nitrite, blood and protein are all negative, it is possible to predict the absence of bacteriuria in more than 50% of urines that are subsequently shown to be culture negative. She obtained a negative predictive value of 90% for total bacterial growth, but a value of 96% for clinically significant growth. This approach can be used to screen out non-infected specimens, and it is discussed in more detail by Dr. N. Lightfoot in a later section (Page 100).

Apart from the above chemically-based screening tests for bacteriuria, a large number of other tests have been proposed. Some of these have a biochemical basis, such as the measurement of ATP, which is quantitatively related to bacterial mass, and gas liquid chromatography which permits the direct identification of certain uropathogens. Yet other screening tests depend on physico-chemical measurements, such as changes in electrical impedance changes or heat production during bacterial growth.

There is no general consensus about the value of these methods of screening for covert bacteriuria. However, there can be little doubt that such methods, in settings where they have been carefully assessed by comparison with standard cultural methods, may be useful in identifying urine specimens that are likely to be culture-negative.

To avoid false positive and false negative results, effective screening requires the use of a series of rapid tests used in combination. A useful combination consists of reagent strip tests for nitrite, pyuria, blood and protein. When all these tests are negative, it can safely be assumed that infection by the common uropathogens is absent. Screening, therefore, has clear cost advantages in that expensive and labour-intensive tests can be avoided on specimens that are unlikely to reveal anything to the advantage of the patient. Conversely, specimens that give results indicative of infection can be acted upon quickly and examined with greater care. There are advantages here for the patient, the doctor and other health-care personnel, as well as the NHS itself.

*Expensive and labour-intensive tests can be avoided. Specimens indicative of infection can be acted on quickly and examined with greater care*

## 4.1  Screening for UTI

Screening for any disease has both ethical and financial implications. Screening is ethical only if effective and useful treatment is available, and it is justifiable only if the cost of screening and treatment are cost-effective when balanced against expenditure on medical treatment as a whole. This makes it necessary to take into account the cost of treating the potential complications of the condition for which screening is proposed. On this basis, screening for covert bacteriuria fulfils no useful purpose except in pregnancy, where acute pyelonephritis (APN) can be effectively prevented. The same may be true in children with vesico-ureteric reflux. However, since vesico-ureteric reflux cannot be screened for by non-invasive means, screening for covert bacteriuria in children requires intensive follow-up and control, and is costly.

Generally speaking, screening for significant bacteriuria would predominantly identify individuals with covert bacteriuria. Since covert bacteriuria is harmless in the absence of other predisposing factors, screening for it is pointless. Moreoever, the high relapse and re-infection rates after antimicrobial treatment of covert bacteriuria[4] makes it unlikely that acute UTI can be prevented in this way. In any case, the treatment of acute UTI in the normal urinary tract is highly effective.

Screening may be justified in special circumstances where UTI is difficult or impossible to identify on the basis of clinical criteria alone, or where the early diagnosis and/or prevention of UTI affords significant benefits (*Table 2*). Thus, screening may be useful in infants where "failure to thrive" may be due to UTI and its timely treatment may prevent renal damage. Similarly in pregnancy – where there is a strong association between covert bacteriuria and the development of acute pyelonephritis – periodic screening during antenatal examination is valuable. When covert bacteriuria is found during pregnancy, treatment and follow-up are indicated. Screening is also useful in special risk groups such as diabetics, after catheterisation, urological surgery or invasive urological investigations. Finally, it has been suggested but not satisfactorily confirmed, that covert bacteriuria in the elderly is associated with a reduced life expectancy. When confirmed, this may constitute an important indication for screening.

| Table 2 |
| --- |
| **Appropriate Screening Groups for U.T.I.** |
| <ul><li>"Failure to thrive" infants</li><li>Children with Vesico-Ureteric Reflux</li><li>Pregnancy</li><li>Post catheterisation</li><li>Post-urological surgery or invasive investigation</li><li>Elderly?</li></ul> |

### 5. THE NATURAL HISTORY OF UTI

Our understanding of the natural history of UTI is based on two amply confirmed facts. First, that the infecting organisms derive almost exclusively from the commensal bowel flora of the patient, and second, that the infecting organisms usually enter via the urethra and that the resulting infections are ascending. Haematogenous ("descending") infections will not be considered in the context of this discussion.

An important determining factor for the behaviour of uropathogenic bacteria in the urinary tract is urine, which supports their growth. This conclusion is based on "in-vitro" observations and the surprising fact that UTI does not occur in the anuric urinary tract. The probable reason is that the urothelium has powerful antibacterial mechanisms.

In terms of the mechanisms that permit bacteria to infect the urinary tract, most is known about *Escherichia coli*, but it is reasonable to assume that similar mechanisms apply to other bacteria. Some strains of *E. coli* possess a series of specific adhesive structures, termed fimbriae (*Figure 2*), which allow the organisms to adhere to cells that bear the necessary receptors. These fimbriae are classified according to the nature of the receptor to which they attach. The fimbriae most widely distributed amongst Gram-negative bacteria attach to mannose-containing molecules. Others attach to the P blood group and related substances, M and S blood group substances (glycophorins). Other fimbrial receptors of uropathogenic *E. coli* have yet to be identified. It is likely that by means of fimbrial adhesions, bacteria first colonise the periurethral area and then the urethra itself. It is thought that during the initial stages of the ascent to the urinary tract, the mannose-dependent fimbriae are involved and that at some stage, possibly in the upper urethra, a switch takes place to non-mannose-dependent fimbriae. The latter are known to be important determinants of uropathogenicity, and the former are not produced when bacterial growth takes place in the absence of urine.

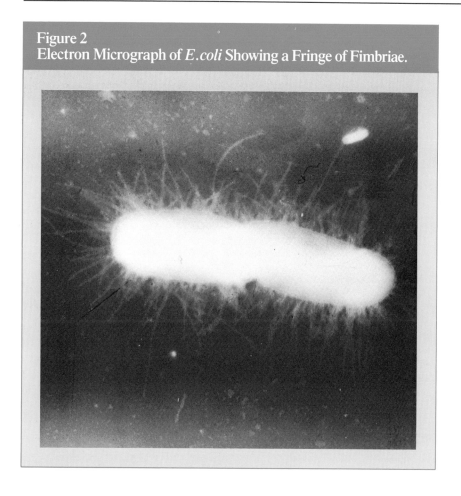

**Figure 2**
**Electron Micrograph of *E.coli* Showing a Fringe of Fimbriae.**

Once the organisms have reached the bladder, they adhere to the urothelium and produce the inflammation associated with cystitis. This is accompanied by an increased rate of shedding of bladder epithelial cells, to which large numbers of bacteria are attached. The mechanisms of these phenomena are unknown.

The precise manner in which infection ascends to the upper urinary tract to produce acute pyelonephritis is unknown. However, in pregnancy – when this course of events is relatively common – the upper urinary tract is dilated, probably because of the pressure exerted by the gravid uterus, a situation akin to obstructive uropathy. In addition, the pH of the urine in pregnancy is raised, and this would tend to encourage the growth of urinary pathogens. Outside pregnancy it must be assumed that unknown factors occasionally prevail, which encourage or permit bacteria to reach and invade the renal parenchyma. There is evidence that fimbriae specific for P blood group receptors are important in this process, especially in children.

Chronic pyelonephritis in the adult does not develop in the structurally and functionally normal urinary tract

The pathogenesis of chronic pyelonephritis (CPN) has long been a subject of interest, and it is now possible to present a credible account of its natural history. The first essential fact to note is that CPN does not, in adult life, develop in the structurally and functionally normal urinary tract. It may, however, develop at any age in the presence of obstructive uropathy or in the so-called "urogenic" bladder associated with paraparesis. It is now generally accepted that the origins of CPN are to be found in early life, when UTI is frequently accompanied by vesico-ureteric reflux. In this situation, the backward pressure up to the ureter is frequently sufficient to lead to reflux of urine into the renal collecting ducts (intrarenal reflux). The reflux of infected urine leads to tissue damage, resulting in the calyectasis and scarring that are the hallmark of chronic pyelonephritis.

*The origins of chronic pyelonephritis are to be found in early life, from the reflux of infected urine*

Little is known about the pathogenesis of covert bacteriuria (CBU), but it is reasonable to assume that the general mechanism is at least similar to that described above. The absence of symptoms in covert bacteriuria may be accounted for by the absence or loss of factors essential for virulence. However this may not be the whole story, because under certain circumstances, as in pregnancy, covert bacteriuria may progress to acute UTI.

*In pregnancy, covert bacteriuria may progress to acute UTI*

## 6. EPIDEMIOLOGY OF UTI

UTI is a very common condition, and we have already noted that it may be covert or symptomatic. In very general terms, after early infancy the *prevalence* of UTI increases throughout life (*Table 3*), with the prevalence in females exceeding that in males. Thus, in infants the prevalence of covert bacteriuria is of the order of 0.001%. In schoolgirls it is on average about 2% and in schoolboys it is about 0.03%. In women, covert bacteriuria has a general prevalence of some 5% between the ages of 21 and 65, rising from about 2.5% at the age of 30 to about 10% at the age of 60. Since it is known that pregnancy potentially affects the overall severity of UTI but not its prevalence, the prevalence of covert bacteriuria in pregnant women is the same, age for age, as that for non-pregnant women. In adult males the prevalence of covert bacteriuria is about 0.5%.

*The prevalence of covert bacteriuria in women is about 2.5% at age 30, rising to about 10% at 60*

*Pregnancy affects the severity of UTI but not the prevalence*

## Table 3
## The Prevalence of Covert Bacteriuria

|  | Age in Years | Mean % Prevalence |
|---|---|---|
| Infants | Premature | 3 |
| Infants | Neonates | 1 |
| Infants | 0–5 | 0.001 |
| Schoolboys | 5–12 | 0.03 |
| Schoolboys | 5 | 1.5 |
| Schoolgirls | 5–12 | 2 |
| Adult males | 21–65 | 0.5 |
| Adult females | 21–65 | 5 |
| Adult females | 35–54 | 2.5 |
| Adult females | 55–65 | 10 |

Studies in general practice in the UK in 1981/82 have shown that the consultation rate per 1000 persons at risk for cystitis and UTI is 14 for males and 62 for females, a female to male ratio of 4–5:1. Thus, in a practice of, say 2500 patients, there are likely to be some 95 consultations for UTI annually.

Little is known about the annual *incidence* of UTI. In schoolgirls the incidence has been estimated at 0.4% per annum. On general grounds it has been estimated that at least 20% of women can expect to experience UTI in their lifetime.

*At least 20% of women can expect to experience UTI*

The pattern of annual consultation rates is shown in *Figure 3*, and the incidence rates are shown in *Figure 4*.

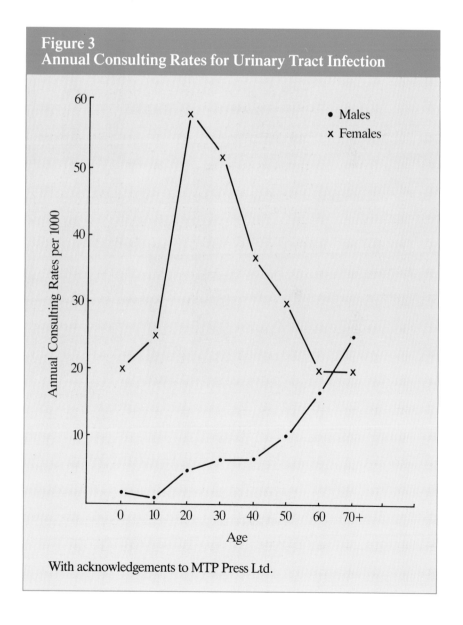

## Figure 3
## Annual Consulting Rates for Urinary Tract Infection

With acknowledgements to MTP Press Ltd.

59

Figure 4
Incidence Rates of Cystitis and Urinary Tract Infection in
General Practice (after: Morbidity Statistics in General Practice.
Third National Study 1981-82. HMSO, 1986)

Figure 4
Incidence Rates of Cystitis and Urinary Tract Infection in
General Practice (after: Morbidity Statistics in General Practice.
Third National Study 1981-82. HMSO, 1986)

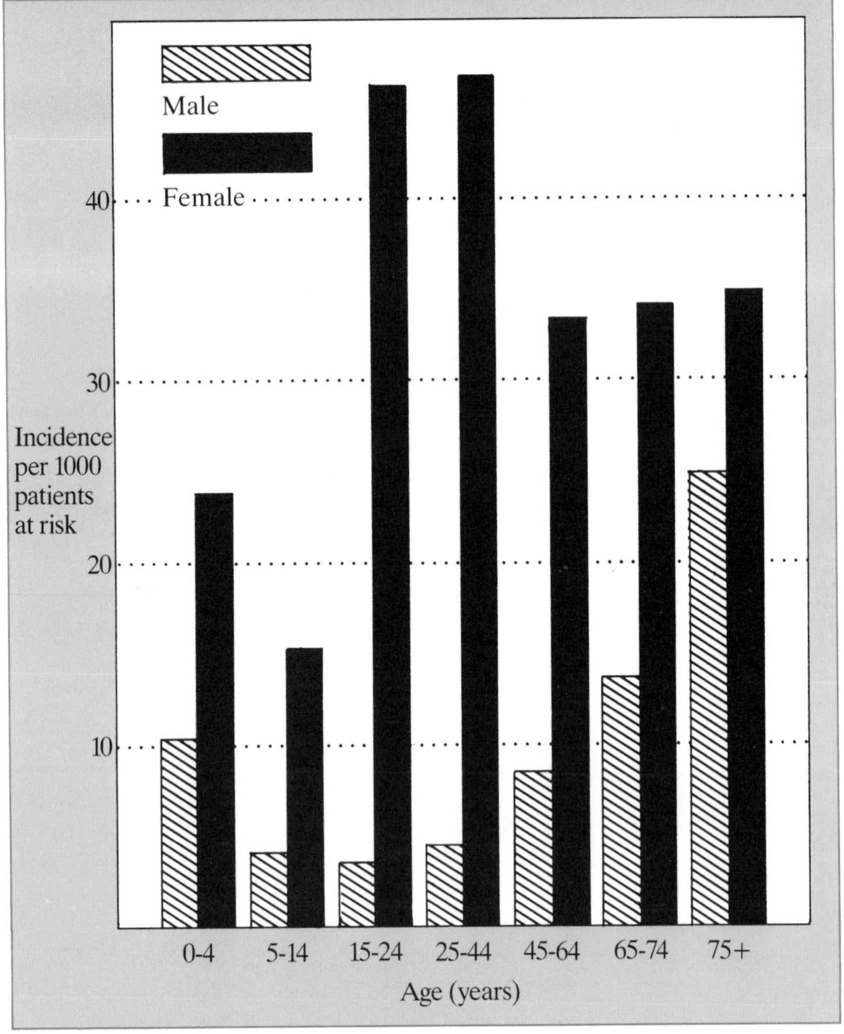

## 7. TREATMENT AND PROPHYLAXIS

Treatment of acute uncomplicated UTI is a straightforward matter, but
reinfection or relapse are not uncommon. Such recurrences are usually equally
easily managed, but it is a matter for clinical judgement when recurrences
should lead to further investigation.

Generally, the organisms responsible for acute UTI – except when these are
hospital acquired – are sensitive to most commonly used drugs. When the

infection turns out to be refractory to treatment, predisposing factors in the patient are likely to be the cause rather than resistance of the infecting organism.

It is not appropriate here to enter into the details of possible treatment regimens. However, whichever drug is chosen, its concentration in the urine usually exceeds the minimal inhibitory concentration required to control the infection. Courses of treatment longer than five days are rarely indicated. Indeed, all the evidence suggests that much shorter courses will often suffice.

Prophylaxis of infection may be indicated when recurrences are frequent and there are not treatable underlying factors to account for the recurrences. A suppressive regimen may be indicated in children with recurrent infection associated with reflux, when recurrent UTI is associated with anatomical abnormalities at any age, or in pregnant women with a history of recurrent UTI. Such suppressive treatment requires considerable instruction and discipline; it consists of a combination of high fluid intake, frequent voiding and low dose chemotherapy at night.

## 8. COMPLICATIONS

Most UTI remains localised to the bladder. The commonest complication is probably ascent of the infection to the kidney, with the development of acute pyelonephritis. In practice, there is usually no warning of this by way of a preceding cystitis, and acute pyelonephritis appears out of the blue. However, based on knowledge of covert bacteriuria and its consequences in pregnancy, the assumption is justified that acute pyelonephritis may be preceded at least by a short period of covert bacteriuria.

In the male, infection may spread to the prostate or epididymis.

*Proteus* and some other urinary pathogens produce a urease which, by breaking down urea to ammonia, markedly raises the pH of urine, leading to precipitation of magnesium ammonium phosphate. This may cause stone formation and, indeed, this is almost always the origin of stag-horn calculi.

The commonest source of the E.coli responsible for septicaemia is the urinary tract

The most hazardous, but fortunately unusual, complication of UTI is septicaemia, which has a substantial mortality. Indeed, the commonest source of the *E.coli* responsible for septicaemia is the urinary tract.

### References

1.  Kass, E.H. Asymptomatic infections of the urinary tract. Transactions, American Association of Physicians (1956); **69**: 56–63.

2.  Sussman, M., and Asscher, A.W. Urinary tract infection. in: Renal Disease (Eds. D. Black and N.F. Jones) Blackwell Scientific Publications, Oxford (1979) pp.400–436.

3.  Lowe, P.A. Chemical screening and prediction of bacteriuria – a new approach. Med. Lab. Sci. (1986); **43**: 28–33.

4.  Asscher, A.W., Sussman, M., et al. Asymptomatic significant bacteriuria in the non-pregnant woman. II. Response to treatment and follow-up. Brit. Med. J. (1969); **1**: 804–806.

# Bile Pigments

## Dr. G. Walker
Chemical Pathologist, University Hospital, Nottingham

The two main bile pigments are bilirubin and urobilinogen; urobilinogen is a degradation product of bilirubin.

### BILIRUBIN FORMATION AND TURNOVER

Bilirubin is the end-product of the metabolism of haem. It is synthesised in reticuloendothelial (RE) cells and excreted into the bile.

The processes involved in the formation and turnover of bilirubin are outlined in *Figure 1*. They will be discussed under the following headings:
– Synthesis
– Transport
– Uptake by the liver
– Conjugation
– Excretion
– Degradation
– Absorption of urobilinogen

### 1. Synthesis

*Bilirubin is formed mainly from haemoglobin liberated as a result of breakdown of red blood cells*

*Bilirubin* is an end-product of the metabolism of haem. In health, approximately 85% of bilirubin is produced in reticulo-endothelial (RE) cells in the spleen, bone marrow and liver from *haemoglobin* liberated by the breakdown of erythrocytes. Most of the remainder is formed from haemoglobin liberated from precursor cells which fail to develop into reticulocytes and mature erythrocytes, which are destroyed in the marrow by a process known as ineffective erythropoiesis.

In diseases characterised by excessive haemoglobin turnover because of decreased erythrocyte survival, bilirubin production is increased – this may be due to acquired extrinsic factors including auto-immune processes, or to inborn intrinsic factors. Examples of the latter include membrane abnormalities, such as hereditary serocytosis, enzyme variants such as glucose-6-phosphate dehydrogenase variants, or abnormal haemoglobins, such as HbS in sickle cell disease. Increased bilirubin production due to excessive ineffective erythropoeisis is most commonly due to thalassaemias and megaloblastic anaemias.

### 2. Transport

*Newly synthesised bilirubin is rendered soluble by binding to albumin in plasma, for transport to the liver*

Bilirubin is virtually insoluble in water and, on entering the circulation from the reticulo-endothelial cells in which it is produced, is rendered soluble by being bound to albumin. In healthy adults, only 0.01% is present in plasma in the free or unbound state. Bilirubin in transit between tissue of origin and the liver is described as "unconjugated" or "indirect" – the latter term being derived from the reaction with diazotised sulphanilic acid, which takes place very slowly unless an accelerator such as methanol or caffeine is added.

*Unconjugated bilirubin is not excreted into the urine*

Unconjugated bilirubin is not excreted into the urine; however, being lipid-soluble, the unbound fraction is able to cross cell membranes. When present in high concentration because of saturation of the binding capacity of albumin in plasma (particularly in association with intercurrent conditions such as anoxia and infection), it becomes concentrated in parts of the brain in neonates (*kernicterus*), causing irreversible damage. The risk of kernicterus is increased

Figure 1
Outline of Bilirubin Turnover

**1  Synthesis from haem**

 From haemoglobin

- Effete erythrocytes
- Ineffective erythropoeisis

 From other haem compounds

**2  Transport in plasma bound to albumin**

**3  Uptake by liver**

 Dissociation from albumin and entry into hepatocytes

 Immobilisation by binding to ligandin and protein Z

**4  Conjugation with glucuronic acid**

**5  Excretion of conjugated bilirubin into bile**

**6  Degradation in gut – formation of urobilinogen**

**7  Absorption of some urobilinogen**

 Mostly cleared by liver

 Some excreted into urine

when the plasma albumin concentration is low, and by the administration of drugs such as sulphasoxisole – which displace unconjugated bilirubin from binding sites on albumin molecules. The danger level depends on gestational age, plasma albumin concentration, intercurrent illness and drug treatment. Prevention of kernicterus in infants with high plasma bilirubin concentrations requires reduction of the concentration of unconjugated bilirubin – either by exchange transfusion when the risk is particularly high, or by phototherapy when it is less serious. Photodegradation of bilirubin results in the formation of products which, being water-soluble, are excreted into the urine and do not enter brain cells.

### 3. Uptake by Liver

Unconjugated bilirubin released from binding by albumin enters parenchymal liver cells (hepatocytes) and is immobilised by being bound to two proteins – ligandin and protein Z. Impaired bilirubin uptake and subnormal concentration of intracellular binding proteins are factors in the pathogenesis of Gilbert's syndrome. This is a group of conditions in which a modestly raised concentration of unconjugated bilirubin is found in plasma in the absence of over-production of bilirubin or of evidence of other hepatocyte dysfunction. The plasma bilirubin concentration in these patients is reduced by the administration of phenobarbitone, which is known to increase the concentration of ligandin and protein Z in hepatocytes.

### 4. Conjugation

Bilirubin is made water-soluble by conjugation with glucuronic acid in hepatocytes. The reaction is mediated by the enzyme UDP-glucuronyl transferase. Conjugated bilirubin is sometimes known as "direct" bilirubin because, unlike unconjugated or "indirect" bilirubin, it reacts promptly with diazotised sulphanilic acid in the absence of an accelerating agent. Conjugated bilirubin is excreted into the urine when present in the plasma in excessive concentration. In health, very little conjugated bilirubin is found in plasma (less than 2 μmol/L out of a total bilirubin concentration of 5–17 μmol/L).

Defective conjugation, with accumulation of unconjugated bilirubin in plasma without excess conjugated bilirubin, is seen in "physiological" jaundice in neonates. This may be due to temporary deficiency of UDP-glucuronyl transferase, and is also seen in some slightly older infants fed on breast milk which contains an enzyme inhibitor, and in the mild and complete forms of the Crigler-Najjar syndrome – in which there is an inborn deficiency or absence, respectively, of enzyme activity. It is also found in association with excess conjugated bilirubin in acute and in some cases chronic hepatitis. Cirrhosis – a condition in which there is a reduced number of hepatocytes – also leads to defective conjugation.

### 5. Excretion

Conjugated bilirubin is excreted into the bile together with bile salts, cholesterol and other solutes. Accumulation with reflux into plasma occurs as mentioned above when there is injury to hepatocytes, as well as when there is an obstruction to the biliary tract. Biliary tract obstruction may be intrahepatic e.g. due to an adverse reaction to drugs, or extrahepatic, e.g. due to gallstones or carcinoma of the pancreas, or occasionally due to an isolated transport defect in patients with the Dubin-Johnson or the Rotor syndrome.

When present in excess in plasma, some conjugated bilirubin becomes firmly bound to albumin and is known as "delta bilirubin". This is cleared from the circulation only slowly, which explains the slow resolution of jaundice in some patients after successful relief of biliary tract obstruction. Delta bilirubin is not excreted into the urine.

### 6. Degradation

Bilirubin is deconjugated and reduced in the colon in reactions mediated by enzymes present in micro-organisms. The resulting series of compounds is known collectively as *urobilinogen* (or stercobilinogen). Most of the urobilinogen in the colon undergoes spontaneous oxidation and is excreted as urobilin (or stercobilin), giving the characteristic brown colour to faeces.

### 7. Absorption of Urobilinogen

Some urobilinogen is absorbed into the blood, from which it is cleared by the liver. Any which escapes clearance is excreted into the urine. In a healthy adult, the urinary output of urobilinogen is less than 5mg/day out of a total production of the order of 300mg/day.

Excess urobilinogen is found in urine in association with increased bilirubin turnover in haemolytic conditions and when there is excessive destruction of precursor red blood cells (ineffective erythropoiesis). It is also seen in conditions in which there is impairment of hepatocyte function and/or reduction in the number of hepatocytes. In patients with complete biliary tract obstruction, lack of bilirubin in the colon results in loss of the normal colour of faeces, which become pale, and also in the absence of urobilinogen from the urine.

### JAUNDICE

Jaundice is caused by generalised accumulation of bilirubin in tissues, including skin and sclera, secondary to a high concentration of bilirubin in plasma (hyperbilirubinaemia). The skin colour differs according to whether jaundice is due to accumulation of unconjugated or conjugated bilirubin. In the former case the colour is typically a bright lemon yellow, whilst accumulation of conjugated bilirubin gives a duller shade of yellow.

A classification of jaundice based on defects in bilirubin turnover is given in *Table 1*.

Elucidating the type of jaundice is an essential preliminary to determining its cause in individual patients. Tests for bilirubin and excess urobilinogen in urine are particularly important. A negative test for bilirubin indicates that jaundice is due to accumulation of unconjugated bilirubin, whilst a positive result reflects the presence of excess conjugated bilirubin in plasma. In patients who do not yet show symptoms of jaundice, finding bilirubinuria without excess urinary urobilinogen may lead to the early diagnosis of viral hepatitis.

These tests may be conveniently performed in the surgery, hospital or home using reagent strip tests such as MULTISTIX* 10SG, or the reagent tablet test ICTOTEST, which is specific for bilirubin and is more sensitive than the strip

**Table 1**
**Types of Jaundice**

**Overproduction of bilirubin (Pre-hepatic)**

- Haemolytic disorders
- Ineffective erythropoeisis

**Hepatocyte disorders**

- Congenital hyperbilirubinaemias
- Acquired disorders

**Biliary tract obstruction**

- Congenital atresia
- Acquired – intra-hepatic
            extra-hepatic

*In acute viral hepatitis, bilirubinuria characteristically preceeds the excretion of excess urobilinogen and the appearance of jaundice*

test. Therefore, reagent strip testing may suggest viral hepatitis before symptoms appear. Indications for testing for bilirubin and excess urobilinogen in urine are listed in *Table 2*.

**Table 2**
**Indications for Testing for Bilirubin and Excess Urobilinogen in Urine**

- Differential diagnosis of jaundice (see *Table 3*)

- Initial investigation of patients in whom liver disease is suspected or possible
    - Lassitude, nausea, vomiting which might be due to pre-icteric viral hepatitis
    - Heavy ethanol intake
    - Exposure to hepatotoxic chemicals or natural products
    - Stigmata of chronic liver disease, including vascular spiders, foetor, encephalopathy, ascites, oedema

- Confirmation of haemolysis

It is possible to measure concentrations of unconjugated and conjugated bilirubin in plasma or serum, but in practice this is rarely necessary provided urine tests are performed, and most laboratories routinely report results for total (unconjugated + conjugated) bilirubin concentrations. The results of measurements of the activity of certain enzymes in plasma provides further information required to delineate the type of jaundice, as shown in *Table 3*.

Additional investigations including haematological tests for haemolysis, biopsy for chronic liver disease and ultrasonography and radiology for biliary tract obstruction may be required to make a definitive diagnosis.

## Table 3
## Delineation of the Type of Jaundice

| | Bilirubin Overproduction | Acquired Hepatocyte Disorder | Biliary Tract Obstruction |
|---|---|---|---|
| **Urine tests** | | | |
| Bilirubin | − | + | + |
| Urobilinogen | ↑ | ↑ | ↓ |
| **Activity of enzymes in serum** | | | |
| Alanine and/or Asparate Aminotransferase | ± | ↑ | + or ↑ |
| Alkaline Phosphatase | ± | Variable | ↑ |
| Gamma Glutamyl Transferase | ± | Variable | ↑ |

**The Effects of Drugs on Bilirubin Production**

Bilirubin production is increased in individuals when drugs cause haemolysis. Certain drugs, particularly penicillin and methyldopa, cause haemolysis in susceptible individuals by immunological mechanisms; drug-induced haemolysis also occurs in individuals with glucose 6P-DH variants, when it is most often precipitated by analgesics, antimalarials and antibiotics.

# Urine Analysis in Paediatrics

**Dr. I. G. Jefferson**
Consultant Paediatrician, Hull Royal Infirmary

### Introduction

Although modern clinical biochemistry focuses particularly on the analysis of plasma or serum factors, routine urine analysis can often provide valuable clinical data and has the obvious advantage, in paediatric practice, that its collection is painless. Even in small babies, urine can be relatively easily collected using the "clean catch technique" by the adept nurse or clinician; or the use of sterile perineal collection bags (most useful in the male with advantageous anatomy). Urine can also be collected by extraction from the nappy or a cotton wool ball placed in the nappy; however, interpretation of this latter "dirty" technique should be treated with caution. Where the above methods fail and a sterile sample is essential, a supra-pubic needle aspiration can be undertaken in babies, although this of course is not painless.

### Glycosuria

The presence of glucose in urine may be detected by either a reducing method (e.g. CLINITEST* reagent tablets) – which will detect any reducing sugar – or by an enzymatic method which is specific for glucose (such as DIASTIX* reagent strip tests).

*The reducing test CLINITEST and not the enzymatic methods must be used to screen for galactose in the neonatal period*

In the neonatal period, the presence of prolonged jaundice should prompt the testing of urine for reducing sugars with CLINITEST to exclude the inherited disorder of galactosaemia. If present, this would necessitate the withdrawal of lactose-containing milk feeds whilst awaiting more specific diagnosis based on urine chromatography and enzyme assays. In the neonatal period, the sick baby is often unable to metabolise glucose at the rates and concentrations of standard intravenous regimes. This tendency is magnified in neonates and also in older children who require parenteral nutrition. Therefore, urine from neonates on intravenous fluids and older children on parenteral nutrition, should be regularly tested for glucose to detect glycosuria and its consequent risk of osmotic diuresis and dehydration.

In later childhood, the presence of glycosuria most commonly indicates the presence of insulin dependent diabetes. However, glycosuria may also be present in other conditions such as physiologically low renal glucose threshold, renal tubular disorders, at times of severe stress such as following a grand-mal convulsion, and in children on high dose steroid therapy. The finding of glycosuria in children always warrants further investigation in terms of blood glucose estimation, and occasionally formal glucose tolerance testing may be necessary.

Insulin dependent diabetes in children is not an uncommon disease, with an age-specific incidence of around 18 per 100,000 per year, giving an age-specific prevalence of around 1 in 600 in the 0–18 year age group. The incidence of this disease may well be increasing. With current clinical awareness, most children are diagnosed before they reach the stage of ketoacidosis, presenting with the classical triad of symptoms and signs of polyuria, polydipsia and weight loss.

It is important not to miss early opportunities of diagnosis, and children presenting with secondary nocturnal enuresis should always have their urine tested for glucose in addition to screening for urinary infection. A random urine sample during the day is often more reliable than an early morning specimen, since in the early stages of the development of diabetes, children may have

All children with a
suspected new diagnosis
of insulin dependent
diabetes mellitus should
have same-day referral to
a paediatrician

normal fasting blood glucose values without glycosuria. Any child found to
have glycosuria requires blood glucose estimation and preferably same-day
referral to a paediatrician as, although the child may still be clinically well, if
they have diabetes mellitus a simple intercurrent illness can quickly push them
into ketoacidosis. It is obviously preferable to make the diagnosis and undertake
initial management in a well child, rather than have the upset and risk of
intensive treatment for ketoacidosis. Diabetic ketoacidosis can often present
with abdominal pain and mimic the "acute abdomen"; all children presenting
with the possibility of a surgical acute abdomen should have urine tested for
glucose and ketones before surgery. This simple test avoids the often fatal
tragedy of unnecessary surgery on the newly presenting child with diabetes.

## Table 1
## Indications for Glycosuria Testing in Paediatrics

**Reducing Sugars**

CLINITEST + confirmatory test for galactosaemia in prolonged
jaundice

**Glucose**

Diagnosis of Insulin Dependent Diabetes Mellitus

Ketoacidosis

"Acute abdomen"

Osmotic diuresis and dehydration, during intravenous fluids and
parenteral nutrition

Low renal threshold

Renal tubular disorders

Severe stress

### Ketonuria

Children should test
for urine ketones if
their blood glucose
concentration exceeds
12 mmol/L

Urine testing for ketones is important for a rapid diagnosis of ketoacidosis. In
addition to blood glucose testing, children with diabetes should test their urine
for ketones if they are hyperglycaemic. Many children with diabetes have
erratic blood glucose control, and should test their urine for ketones if they have
a random blood glucose concentration of 18mmol/L or greater, or if they have a
persistent hyperglycaemia of 12mmol/L or more. The presence of ketonuria is
indicative of a more severe or prolonged relative lack of insulin rather than a
transient hyperglycaemia. Similarly, the presence of ketonuria during
intercurrent illness may indicate a relative lack of insulin.

### Proteinuria

The presence of abnormal proteinuria usually indicates increased glomerular
permeability, the presence of tubular damage or tubular inflammation. Benign
postural (orthostatic) proteinuria will occasionally be detected on routine
testing, although this is unusual in young children. The quantity of protein
excreted is usually less than 1.5 grams/24 hours, and this benign condition is
easily identified by the absence of protein from the first-morning sample. Low
levels of benign proteinuria may also be found during any acute febrile episode.

The commonest cause of glomerular proteinuria in children is nephrotic syndrome, and by far the vast majority of these will be "minimal change", steroid-sensitive nephrotic syndrome. The incidence of this is variable, but probably is around 5–10 per 100,000 per year in the childhood age range. The classic presentation is of oedema, proteinuria and hypoalbuminaemia, and regular urine testing is used to monitor the response to treatment and identify any subsequent relapse. Although definitions vary, the presence of "+++" proteinuria for three consecutive days and/or the presence of clinical oedema is considered evidence of relapse requiring further treatment. During relapse, the child is at risk of infection and hypovolaemia – both of which may give rise to abdominal pain simulating the "acute abdomen". This is a further reason for routine urine testing in all children with "acute abdomen" prior to going to theatre – in this case to avoid unnecessary surgery on the relapsed or newly diagnosed nephrotic, who may have primary peritonitis or mesenteric ischaemia due to hypovolaemia.

Tubular proteinuria may be a feature of various paediatric diseases such as cystinosis, Wilson's disease, Low's syndrome and Fanconi's syndrome.

The nephropathic complications of insulin dependent diabetes do not often present in childhood, but proteinuria should be looked for routinely. There is some evidence that the detection of low levels of proteinuria, possibly in relation to exercise stress testing, may be able to identify people at risk of diabetic nephropathy at an earlier and treatable stage of their disease. Although detection of these low levels of albuminuria usually requires laboratory urine testing by radioimmunoassay or immunoturbidimetric techniques, there is now a semi-quantitative clinic test for albumin at low levels in the form of MICRO-BUMINTEST* reagent tablets.

Proteinuria may also be a feature of urinary tract infection (see below).

## Table 2
### Significance of Proteinuria in Paediatrics

- Increased glomerular permeability
  - Nephrotic Syndrome
  - "Acute abdomen"

- Renal tubular damage
  - Cystinosis
  - Wilson's disease
  - Low's syndrome
  - Fanconi's syndrome

- Urinary tract infection

- Inflammation

- Micro-albuminuria
  - Early indication of diabetic nephropathy

### Haematuria

Lower urinary tract and local causes of haematuria in children are rare, and the presence of microscopic or macroscopic haematuria in a child warrants further

investigation. It may well accompany urinary infection (see below), but if the
urine is sterile and if the haematuria is persistent, particularly if accompanied by
significant proteinuria, then a glomerulonephritis (most likely post-infectious) is
a likely cause. In this case, careful monitoring of sequential urine analysis, renal
function and blood pressure are required. Although rare, haematuria may also
be a presenting feature of a renal tumour, such as Wilm's tumour.

### Bile Pigments

Although jaundice is a relatively common problem in paediatric practice,
particularly within the neonatal period, urine testing for bile pigments does not
form a major part of investigation. In neonatal physiological and haemolytic
jaundice, bilirubin will be absent from the urine but there will be excess
urobilinogen. In "neonatal hepatitis" (incidence 2–4 per 1,000 live births) or
with viral hepatitis occurring in later childhood, there is often a mixed
obstructive/hepatitic picture. The presence here of bilirubinuria may be a
helpful early finding in the child presenting with vague abdominal pain and
malaise before the presence of hepatitis is clinically detectable.

Bilirubinuria may be a
helpful early finding
before hepatitis is
clinically detectable

### Infection

Large numbers of children present to their General Practitioners and
Paediatricians with urinary symptoms that could be due to infection, but many
of these will have other causes for their symptoms.

Untreated upper urinary
tract infection can lead
to permanent renal
scarring and damage

It is essential that as much as possible is done to get a sound bacteriological
diagnosis before antibiotics are prescribed. However, this does not necessarily
mean waiting for the results, as untreated upper urinary tract infection can lead
to permanent scarring and damage.

Collection of clean urine specimens in small children is very difficult. Where
co-operation is present, strict adherence to the sterile mid-stream technique is
essential; in smaller children, bag or better still, clean-catch samples will suffice,
but in all cases the samples must be transferred to the laboratory as soon as
possible and stored appropriately if any storage time is necessary, to avoid
overgrowth by contaminants. Distinguishing between contamination and
infection is often difficult, even taking into account microscopy for cells and
analysis for protein. This dilemma may be eased by the use of the Nitrite strip
test, but it is also advisable where possible to collect two or three separate
samples before starting antibiotics, so that a consensus of results may be viewed.

All children who are shown to have had definite urinary tract infection deserve
referral for further consideration of urinary tract abnormality and possible
investigation. This is most important, as children with upper tract dilatation
and/or vesico-ureteric reflux merit close follow-up and the use of carefully
monitored "prophylactic antibiotics". Home testing for the follow-up of urinary
infection may not currently be useful, as there is no substitute for culture
and microscopy.

In children found to have asymptomatic bacteriuria, the choice of antibiotic
used in other "intercurrent illness" should be modified, as injudicious use of
antibiotics may cause a harmless "commensal strain" to be replaced by a
pathogenic organism.

### Specific Gravity

Urine specific gravity can be very useful in assessing fluid balance in sick children, especially in the post-operative period. It has been used in the neo-natal intensive care situation, where fluid losses can be extreme – especially if nursed on overhead radiant heaters.

Caution is necessary in interpreting results, as unrecognised glycosuria can give misleadingly high values by traditional methods. More accurate data is obtained by comparing serum and urine osmolalities where available, but with the same caution over abnormal urinary solutes. The urine strip test for Specific Gravity (Ames) has the advantage of not being affected by glycosuria, unlike other more traditional methods of measurement.

### Pyuria

The absence of white cells with a positive culture may indicate contamination

Testing for the presence of white blood cells in the urine is an important adjunct to the finding of a positive urine culture; coupled with the absence of white cells, it suggests possible contamination.

Pyuria in a sterile urine may suggest bacterial suppression by antibiotics

The presence of white blood cells in a sterile urine might indicate bacterial suppression by antibiotic treatment; it may also be found in an acute febrile episode, or if heavy and persistent, should raise the possibility of tuberculosis.

### Conclusions

Urine testing forms an important part of the overall assessment of a child presenting to a doctor or other health workers, whether the presenting symptoms are related to the urinary tract or not. It should form part of the routine for all hospital admissions, and a case can be made for its forming an important and routine part of all consultations in hospitals and at the GP's surgery, certainly on the first visit.

Urine testing at home may form an important part of management and may shorten hospital admission

In specific instances, urine testing at home forms an important part of management, and under the correct circumstances may shorten a hospital in-patient admission. This includes testing for glycosuria in children with diabetes or suspected diabetes; for proteinuria in follow-up of nephrotic syndrome; and for proteinuria and blood in follow-up of the acute phase of mild nephritis and/

or Henoch Schönlein Syndrome. Thus, urine testing forms a simple to perform, non-invasive method of assessing many medical conditions, and allows a cost-effective way of early detection and delineation of many diseases throughout the childhood age range.

# Urine Analysis in the Assessment of Jaundiced Infants

**Dr Alex P. Mowat**
Consultant Paediatric Hepatologist
King's College Hospital, London SE5 9RS

Virtually 100% of infants have serum bilirubin concentrations above the adult range in the first week of life. The bilirubin produces a symptomless yellowing of the skin, sclera and tissues in up to 90%. Factors contributing to the jaundice include:

a) excessive bilirubin production: from red cells which have a reduced life span in this age group, ineffective erythropoiesis, and rapidly turning over haem-containing enzymes.

b) a transient defect in hepatic uptake of bilirubin.

c) impaired bilirubin conjugation with glucuronic acid.
Which of the many metabolic processes contributing to bilirubin transport and excretion are transiently inefficient is by no means certain.

d) an important additional factor is increased enteric reabsorption of bilirubin. Such jaundice is usually described as *physiological*[1,2,3].

Until recently it was considered that bilirubin was a breakdown product of no physiological importance. Elegant studies have now shown that it acts as a potent antioxidant which may assume physiological importance, particularly when plasma ascorbic acid is decreased[4,5]. Such jaundice appears on the second or third day of life, and usually clears by the seventh day in full-term infants and by fourteen days in pre-term infants. Although for the last forty years it has been shown that bilirubin in high concentrations causes permanent brain damage, how it does this remains unclear. This brain damage only occurs with very high serum bilirubin concentrations exceeding the capacity of binding proteins in serum, particularly albumin, to bind circulating bilirubin firmly[5,6].

*Bilirubin acts as a potent antioxidant of physiological importance*

It is important to appreciate that such physiological jaundice can be aggravated by a range of pathological processes. These include systemic infections, haemolytic diseases and metabolic disorders, as well as diseases of the liver and biliary tract (*Table 1*). These conditions have an appreciable morbidity and mortality if diagnosis is delayed.

*Pathological conditions aggravating physiological jaundice may have an appreciable morbidity and mortality if diagnosis is delayed*

## Table 1
## Aggravating Factors for Physiological Jaundice

- Systemic infections
- Haemolytic disease
- Metabolic disorders
- Liver disease
- Biliary tract disease

*Urine analysis* is an essential part of the examination of infants in whom jaundice is in any way atypical:

- jaundice in the first twenty-four hours of life

- jaundice in an infant who is otherwise ill

*Urine analysis is essential if jaundice is in any way atypical*

- jaundice which has spread to the lower abdomen or thighs (which is a crude guide that the bilirubin is greater than 200μmol/L and that accurate biochemical testing is essential), indicating a concentration above that found in physiological jaundice

- jaundice persisting beyond fourteen days of age

- jaundice with yellow urine

Urinalysis should include testing for the bile pigments bilirubin and urobilinogen, using reagent strip tests such as BILI-LABSTIX* or MULTISTIX* 10SG; reducing substances both with CLINITEST* tablets and with glucose oxidase reagent strips to identify the presence of non-glucose-reducing substances (see below); as well as testing for haematuria (see below) and proteinuria (*Table 2*). Urine microscopy and culture is also essential in the infant who is unwell.

Given these circumstances, urine analysis provides essential diagnostic information complementing that obtained from the history and physical examination. Other laboratory investigations, particularly blood culture, full blood count, blood group determination, investigations for deficiencies of red cell enzymes or abnormalities of red blood cell membrane, serum thyroxine (T4), thyroid stimulating hormone (TSH) concentrations and serial determination of the total and direct serum bilirubin may be necessary.

**Jaundice in an Infant More Than Fourteen Days of Age**

*Urine testing will show the presence of bile pigments, indicating conjugated jaundice*

It is essential to decide whether such jaundice is unconjugated or conjugated. In the latter, urine analysis (using ICTOTEST*) will show the presence of bile pigment in the urine, except in the very late stages of liver disease. Laboratory analysis will show a high serum bilirubin with over 30% direct reacting. If there is no bile pigment in the urine, five main differential diagnoses need to be considered:

1. Persistence of factors aggravating physiological jaundice, e.g. persistent haemolysis, infection.

2. *Hypothyroidism*
   This may occur with or without a goitre. There may be a family history of hypothyroidism. If it is due to defects in the thyroid gland, the concentration of thyroid-stimulating hormone in the circulation is increased while serum thyroxin is low. If due to pituitary disease, there is no increase in TSH.

   In many developed countries, infants are screened for hypothyroidism by measuring the TSH concentration in the circulation as part of the neonatal screening programme for metabolic disorders such as phenylketonuria. It is important to appreciate that this will not detect hypothyroidism secondary to hypopituitarism.

3. *Breast milk jaundice syndrome*

*Breast feeding may be associated with prolonged unconjugated jaundice in 25%–40% of infants*

Breast feeding may be associated with mild, prolonged hyperbilirubinaemia in between 25% and 40% of infants[6]. It may persist for as long as four months. If breast feeding is stopped, the jaundice will resolve spontaneously within six days and, surprisingly, may not recur if breast feeding is recommenced. The aetiology of this syndrome is unknown. Seventy-five percent of siblings of affected infants develop this syndrome. Breast milk from the mothers of affected infants can be shown to competitively inhibit glucuronide formation in vitro. In addition, milk from such mothers may promote increased enteric reabsorption of bilirubin. This may be related to a high beta-glucuronidase activity.

This appears to be a benign disorder requiring no treatment but reassurance. If the serum bilirubin levels exceed 300µmol/L, breast feeding should be stopped for one to two days to allow the serum bilirubin to fall, and thus obviate any risk of possible kernicterus.

4. *Transient familial hyperbilirubinaemia*
   This rare syndrome causes a persistence of jaundice into the second or third week of life. It appears to be due to an unidentified inhibitor of glucuronide formation which can be recovered from the serum of the mothers and infants. No treatment is required.

5. *Crigler-Najjar syndrome*
   Such jaundice may be due to a disorder characterised by lifelong unconjugated hyperbilirubinaemia due to absence of the enzyme bilirubin uridine diphosphate glucuronyl transferase in the liver. There are two forms of the syndrome. Type 1 is very severe, with serum bilirubin concentrations in the range of 250–750µmol/L. It causes irreversible brain damage (kernicterus), usually in the perinatal period or early infancy, unless treated with exchange transfusion to control the hyperbilirubinaemia immediately, together with intensive phototherapy. This has to be continued for 7–15 hours each night unless liver transplantation is performed.

   *It should be noted that phototherapy, a commonly used treatment for hyperbilirubinaemia in infancy, causes the excretion of yellow bilirubin compounds which have the same appearance as conjugated bilirubin, giving the urine a yellow colour. They do not react, however, with BILI-LABSTIX\*.*

   Type 2 Crigler-Najjar syndrome is characterised by a less severe hyperbilirubinaemia, with serum bilirubin concentrations ranging from 85–340µmol/L, but falling to normal or much lower levels with enzyme-inducing agents such as phenobarbitone. Brain damage is infrequent.

**Conjugated Hyperbilirubinaemia**

Jaundice with bile pigments in the urine indicates significant liver or biliary tract disease. Urgent investigation is required to make an accurate aetiological and structural diagnosis and to institute appropriate therapy[7]. The underlying pathology may be characterised into four main categories:

- parenchymal liver disease
- hypoplasia of the intralobular bile ducts
- disorders of the major intrahepatic bile ducts
- disorders involving the extrahepatic bile ducts

The clinical features rarely give a clue to the underlying pathology or associated abnormality. The majority of infants present with jaundice. Some may present with features of liver disease such as a bleeding diathesis or hypoglycaemia. When jaundice is present the urine is yellow in colour. The stools may have reduced or absent yellow or green bile-derived pigment. There is commonly hepatomegaly and splenomegaly. There may or may not be failure to thrive, ascites or evidence of spontaneous bleeding.

The first priority is to exclude treatable disorders. These include infections such as septicaemia, urinary tract infection, herpes simplex infection, toxoplasmosis, syphilis, listeriosis, tuberculosis and malaria. Dietary-treatable metabolic disorders, such as galactosaemia, fructosaemia and tyrosinaemia must be excluded. The main complication to be feared is intracranial haemorrhage due to abnormal clotting, caused by Vitamin K malabsorption, which may complicate such hepatobiliary disease, whatever the underlying cause.

*Urine analysis* is an essential investigation as outlined in *Table 2.*

a) A positive reaction for bile with BILI-LABSTIX or ICTOTEST establishes the presence of conjugated hyperbilirubinaemia.
b) A positive CLINITEST reaction together with a negative test for DIASTIX or CLINISTIX, which are specific for glucose, indicates that reducing substances other than glucose are present. The presence of non-glucose reducing substances in the urine should lead to a presumptive diagnosis of *galactosaemia.* It is important to appreciate that *galactosuria* in galactosaemia may be intermittent, appearing only after a galactose load, in the same way as the intermittent glucosuria in a patient with mild diabetes mellitus. It is thus essential to collect urine passed within three hours of a galactose load.

## Table 2
## Urine Tests in Jaundiced Babies

- Bile pigments
- Reducing sugars, e.g. Galactose, Fructose
- Glucose
- Blood
- Protein
- Microscopy
- Culture

Galacatosuria occurs in up to one-third of infants admitted to our service for investigation of liver disease in infancy. Only a very small percentage have galactosaemia. The remainder have impaired liver function of such severity that the liver is unable to take up and metabolise to glucose the galactose absorbed following a normal milk feed. The finding of galactosuria is an indication to provide a galactose-free milk, because the effects of not treating galactosaemia are so serious. It is our policy to exclude galactosaemia definitively by measuring galactose-1-phosphate uridyl transferase in red blood cells in all instances.

Non-glucose reducing substances in the urine occur also in *fructosaemia.* Here, a presumptive clinical diagnosis will be made on the dietary history. Breast milk and the vast majority of proprietary artificial milks contain no fructose. Fructose may be given to infants in the form of honey, but more commonly as sweetening agents with medication. The diagnosis of fructosaemia is confirmed by enzymatic analysis on a liver biopsy.

Excessive amino acid excretion in the urine occurs in *tyrosinaemia,* a metabolic disorder with the defect in tyrosine and phenylalanine metabolism. This may be suspected from a positive ferric chloride test in the urine and, more specifically, from the finding of high urinary concentrations of tyrosine, phenylalanine and methionine. The specific diagnosis is usually established by finding high concentrations of the phenylalanine metabolite succinylacetone in the urine. This requires gas-liquid chromatographic techniques. In rare instances excretion of this metabolite is within normal concentrations, and there will be high urinary concentrations of delta aminolaevulinic acid that confirm the diagnosis.

Urinary microscopy for pus cells is essential, as is culture for both bacteria and viruses, particularly cytomegalovirus.

In the assessment of such infants, laboratory investigations will include standard biochemical tests of liver function, prothrombin time to characterise the severity of liver damage, and full blood count. Ultrasonography will be performed to exclude choledochal cysts.

In the absence of a clear guide to the possible cause of liver damage from clinical examination, a systematic scheme of investigation is required to exclude inherited disorders, hormone deficiencies and infections which may present as liver disease in infancy. In all instances galactosaemia, fructosaemia and tyrosinaemia must be excluded since these are treatable metabolic disorders. In the United Kingdom it is essential to exclude alpha-1-antitrypsin deficiency by protease inhibitor phenotyping; cystic fibrosis by determination of sodium or chloride concentrations in sweat; and Niemann-Pick type C disease by bone marrow aspiration, since these conditions have a relatively high prevalence. Such diagnoses have important implications for prognosis and genetic counselling, with early antenatal diagnosis being obtainable. Other lysosomal storage diseases may be suspected on the finding, on liver biopsy, of storage material in the Kupffer cells. Excessive iron deposition may indicate neonatal haemochromatosis.

Hypothyroidism, hypopituitarism, diabetes insipidus, hypoadrenalism and hypoparathyroidism are all possible associated disorders which need to be excluded by specific hormone assays.

As well as the infectious causes of liver disease in infancy mentioned above, for which treatment is available, a whole range of viral infections have been implicated, e.g. rubella, hepatitis A, hepatitis B, non-A non-B hepatitis, herpes simplex, coxsackie A9 and B12, echovirus 12, 11, 14 and 19, adenovirus and reovirus type 3. These need to be excluded by specific serological investigations.

### Surgically Treatable Disorders: Biliary Atresia

By far the most frequent surgically treatable disorder is *extrahepatic biliary atresia* (EHBA). In this disorder, normally formed bile ducts are destroyed by a sclerosing cholangitis. The extrahepatic bile ducts are completely obstructed. The process extends to the ducts within the liver, causing a biliary cirrhosis. The mean age of death of such infants is eleven months[8]. If the affected extrahepatic bile ducts are removed surgically when the bile ducts within the liver substance are patent, long term survival can be achieved[9,10]. In identifying the surgically treatable disorders, ultrasonography will usually identify choledochal cysts, but percutaneous liver biopsy and radio nucleotide investigation of the patency of the biliary tree are required. In extrahepatic biliary atresia, all portal tracts are widened, with oedema, cellular infiltrate, fibrosis and bile duct re-duplication. This is not a specific appearance, being found also in some genetic and endocrine disorders, as well as in a minority of infants who will ultimately develop bile duct hypoplasia. It also occurs in disorders of the intrahepatic bile ducts. The radiopharmaceuticals used in demonstrating bile duct patency are derivatives of iminodiacetic acid (IDA), such as methylbromoida (MBIDA). Following the intravenous injection of technetium-tagged MBIDA, the isotope can be demonstrated in the gut within twenty-four hours if the biliary system is patent and there is adequate hepatic excretion. If it is not excreted into the gut, the histological appearances are those of biliary atresia and genetic disorders have been excluded, laparotomy is indicated as a prelude to corrective surgery.

It is essential that this is undertaken before the infant is eight weeks of age, because then the chances of producing a jaundice-free infant are greater than 80%. With later surgery the success rate falls to around 30%[11]. If the infant's serum bilirubin returns to normal, a 90% ten-year survival has been reported with a good quality of life into the fourth decade. *Unfortunately, the majority of the 35–50 infants who develop this condition in the UK each year have their surgery too late, or have surgery in units in which a good outcome is less likely*[11]. For such children, early death is inevitable unless liver transplantation is available[12,13,14]. This could be avoided if conjugated hyperbilirubinaemia were recognised earlier, and if all those caring for jaundiced infants appreciated the pathological significance of this finding.

Urine testing for bilirubin in these infants is therefore of great importance. Only if this approach is adopted can we reduce the morbidity and mortality associated with the myriad of conditions complicated by conjugated bilirubinaemia. An outline scheme is depicted in *Figure 1*.

## Conclusions

Urine analysis plays a key role in identifying patients with conjugated hyperbilirubinaemia, a finding which is always pathological, as opposed to unconjugated hyperbilirubinaemia, which may be a physiological phenomenon.

It is crucial in providing early evidence that treatable disorders such as galactosaemia and urinary tract infection may be present.

It provides the signpost to appropriate investigation to identify other treatable disorders, and for referral to specialist centres with the diagnostic and surgical skills to provide optimum treatment.

Urine analysis for chemical abnormalities may be conveniently performed by nursing or medical staff. With the modern reagent strips and tablets, results are immediately available and clear-cut. Rational management decisions can then be taken on the basis of having excluded a whole range of disorders, e.g. in unconjugated hyperbililrubinaemia, or of having identified the absolute necessity to undertake further investigations, to identify disorders associated with conjugated hyperbilirubinaemia. The parents thus can then be immediately reassured or re-directed to sources of further advice.

It is difficult to quantify the savings but if, for example, one were to identify conjugated hyperbilirubinaemia with a risk of intracranial bleeding, and then give parenteral vitamin K to prevent this, one could have an intact brain as opposed to an irreparably damaged brain, with all its long-term sequelae. Clearly, the earlier the cause of liver damage can be identified, whether it is due to galactosaemia, urinary tract infection or biliary atresia, the better the outcome of appropriate treatment.

From the figures given above, it is clear that early identification of biliary atresia gives the possibility of long-term survival with an excellent quality of life.

There is, for some infants, associated morbidity due to portal hypertension and recurring cholangitis. This is much, much less than the morbidity associated with liver transplantation, the only other form of management. The mortality associated with liver transplantation is high, with one-year survival rates of between 55% and 85% [14,15]. In the latter series, many will have had two or more transplants. Such patients require very expensive inpatient and intensive care, and require expensive drugs to prevent rejection.

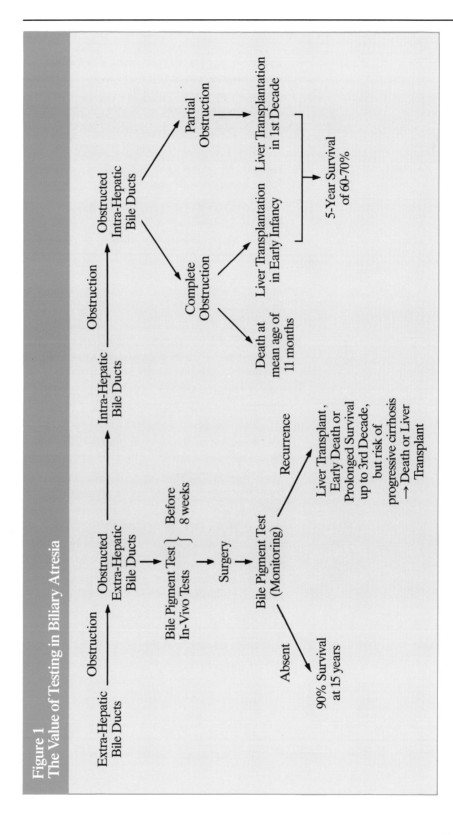

Figure 1
The Value of Testing in Biliary Atresia

## References

1. Levine, R.L. Neonatal jaundice. Acta Paediatr.Scand. (1988); **77**: 177–82.

2. Gollan, J.L., Ed. Pathobiology of Bilirubin and Jaundice. In: Sem.Liv. Disease (1988); **8** (2). Editor-in-Chief Berk P.D. Thieme Medical Publishers Inc, New York. pp1–99.

3. Mowat, A.P. Unconjugated Hyperbililrubinaemia, In: Liver Disorders in Childhood. 2nd Edition (1987), Butterworths, London. p24–36.

4. Perlman, M., Frank, J.W. Bilirubin beyond the blood-brain barrier. Paediatrics (1988); **81**: 304–15.

5. McDonagh, A.F., Lightner, D.A. Phototherapy and the photobiology of bilirubin. Sem.Liv. Disease (1988); **8**: 272–83.

6. Maisels, M.J., Gifford, K., Antle, C.E., Leib, G.R. Jaundice in the healthy newborn infant: A new approach to an old problem. Paediatrics (1988); **81**: 505–11.

7. Mowat, A.P. Hepatitis and cholestasis in infancy: intrahepatic disorders. In: Liver Disorders in Childhood, 2nd edition (1987), Butterworths, London. p37–71.

8. Mowat, A.P. Extra-hepatic biliary atresia and other disorders of the extrahepatic bile ducts presenting in infancy. In: Liver Disorders in Childhood, 2nd edition (1987), Butterworths, London. p72–88.

9. Ohi, R., Hanamatsu, M., Mochizuchi, I., Chiba, T., Kasai, M. Progress in the treatment of biliary atresia. World J. Surg. (1985); **9**: 285–293.

10. Kasai, M., Ohi, R., Chiba, T., Hayashi, Y. A patient with biliary atresia who died 28 years after hepatic portojejunostomy. J.Pediatr.Surg. (1988); **23**: 431–3.

11. Mieli-Vergani, G., Howard, E.R., Portman, B., Mowat, A.P. Late referral for biliary atresia – missed opportunities for effective surgery. Lancet (1989); **i**: 421–3.

12. Stewart, B.A., Hall, R.J., Lilly, J.R. Liver transplantation and the Kasai operation in biliary atresia. J.Pediatr.Surg. (1988); **23**: 623–6.

13. Shaw, B.W., Wood, R.P., Kaufman, S.S., Williams, L., Antonson, D.L., Kelly, D.A., Vanderhoof, J.A. Liver transplant therapy for children (2 parts). J.Pediatr.Gastroenterol.Nutr. (1988); **7**: 157–166 and 797–815.

14. Paradis, K.J.G., Freese, D.K., Sharp, H.L. A Pediatric perspective on liver transplantation. Ped.Clin.N.Am. (1988); **35**: 409–433.

15. Otte, J.B., Yandza, T., Degoyet, J., Tann, K.C., Salizzoni, M., Dehemptinne, B. Paediatrics liver transplantation. Report on 52 patients with a 2-year survival of 86%. J.Paediatr.Surg. (1988); **23**: 250–253.

# Urine Testing in Schools: The Role of the Nurse

**Mrs P. Bolton**

Senior Nurse (Community Child Health), Canterbury and
Thanet DHA, Kent.

### Profile of the Area

Canterbury and Thanet is a mixed area, urban, rural and sociologically. The
coastal towns are favoured by the retired, and the plentiful supply of bed and
breakfast accommodation attracts the homeless. The Thanet end of the District
is more socially deprived and geographically disadvantaged. There is high
unemployment and an increasing incidence of child abuse.

*14% of the population are school children*

The population is approximately 300,000, of whom approximately 42,000 (14%)
are school children. There are approximately 3,000 new entrants to school
every year.

*There are 3,500 children for each school nurse*

We have 100 Primary Schools; 33 Secondary Schools and 12 School Nurses,
i.e. 3,500 children each.

The nurses are geographically based and have their own named schools.
In theory they have a secondary school with its feeder primary schools.
In practice it does not quite work out like that, because we still have selected
places at 11+ and parental choice. Most of the nurses have more than one
secondary school, and some have three.

### Background to the Project

It is common practice in the School Health Service, since the 1944 Education
Act, that all new entrants to school have a medical at school to which the
parents are invited. This medical is conducted by a Clinical Medical Officer
assisted by a school nurse. In our Health Authority, prior to the medical, the
child is screened for hearing, vision, height and weight by the school nurse.

Our Community Consultant Paediatrician considered that the screening could
be enhanced if the child's urine was tested too; she had previously
implemented taking the blood pressure at the medical. Negotiations were
initiated with Ames Division of Miles Ltd, who agreed to support the project.

### Problems

The main problem identified was that of "selling the idea". One had to sell it to:

1.  Health Management – because it was a new development and what were
    the costs?

2.  The Clinical Medical Officers and School Nurses – because of the extra
    work.

3.  Education – because it was new and might involve extra work, especially
    for school secretaries.

4.  Parents – because we needed their co-operation.

Management agreed readily because of the support from Ames, which involved
providing all the bottles, the strips for testing, the forms for the results and use
of their computer to evaluate the results.

The doctors' involvement would be minimal, and only with those children who had abnormalities in the urine; some of those would be referred to the child's General Practitioner. However, they would have to investigate any children who were also enuretic.

---

**Table 1**
**Who to Contact in Setting Up a Urine Testing Programme in School Medicals**

- Health Management
- Clinical Medical Officers
- School Nurses
- Education Authorities
- Schools
- Parents

---

The nurses would have to do the lion's share of the work, and it would be additional to their already busy screening schedule. One or two considered they could not manage extra work, but the majority consented to at least try, especially as it was seen as better screening.

A letter was written to the District Education Officers to be disseminated to the schools, outlining the scheme. The initial reaction from the Head Teachers on the whole was not favourable and in some cases actively hostile. Their main concern seemed to be that there would be urine in bottles in the school setting! Some were also concerned that their secretaries would be involved in extra work. Our Consultant Paediatrician went to several of the Head Teachers' meetings to allay their fears, and eventually they agreed to co-operate when they were told that the nurses would be doing the work, with the minimum of disruption.

It was decided to compose a letter for the parents, explaining about the urine testing and asking for their co-operation. This is never easy, because the intelligence range of the parents is very wide.

### Implementation

Ames personnel conducted a routine training session for the nurses, which included reagent strip urinalysis, interpretation and completing the documentation. The height and weight percentiles and blood pressure were also to be recorded. It was decided that, if any urine abnormalities were found, a second specimen would be obtained the following day and another form would be completed.

*If a urine abnormality was found, a second specimen was requested*

The letters to the parents were put in an envelope with the specimen bottle, and distributed to the children by the nurses the day before their medical. On the day of the medical, the nurse collected the specimens from the parents when they brought the children to school, and they were tested and charted on the child's medical record before the medical session started. If a second specimen was needed, the parent was told by the Clinical Medical Officer when she arrived for the child's medical. All problems were discussed with the parent. This eliminated any involvement by the school staff.

The completed forms were all sent to me. I noted the names of the children who had abnormalities under the appropriate school, and the number tested; I posted them to Ames, who in due course sent us a print-out of the results.

Children with abnormalities were either referred to their General Practitioner or followed up at the School Clinic.

*Children with abnormalities were followed up.*

## Present

As a result of the success in the first Primary School medicals, all children in their first year at Secondary School have their urine tested as part of a screening programme.

*3% of children had an abnormal urinalysis*

Last year we screened 2,423 children. 81 (3%) were found to have abnormalities and were referred. The results are presented and discussed by Dr. Heather Richardson in the next chapter.

## Future

When our Child Health Module is put on our computer, we hope to record the abnormal five-year-olds, so that we can make comparisons with their test at eleven. Screening for abnormalities in the urine is part of our screening programme, and is considered to be cost-effective if it prevents more complex problems later in a child's life.

*Screening for urine abnormalities is cost-effective if it prevents more complex problems later in life*

## Acknowledgement

We are grateful to Ames for giving us the opportunity to enhance our screening programme, for their co-operation and collation of the results.

# Urine Testing in Schools: Clinical Considerations

**Dr. H. Richardson**

Consultant Paediatrician (Community Child Health), Canterbury and Thanet DHA, Kent.

### Introduction

The School Health Service in Canterbury and Thanet runs a school medical for five-year-old children. It was decided to introduce urine screening as a part of this service.

### Aims and Objectives

1. To look at the feasibility of parents and children collecting early morning urine samples and bringing them to the school premises.

2. To use the school nurse to test urine, using Ames reagent strip tests.

3. To record pH and identify the presence of protein, blood, ketones, glucose and nitrite (evidence of infection) in the early morning urines.

4. To measure height and blood pressure of the children. This aspect will not be discussed here.

5. To identify from this prospective study, the specific rate by age and sex for occurrence of proteinuria, haematuria, glycosuria, nitrite and ketonuria in early morning specimens of five-year-old school entrants, and to identify early chronic pathology in childhood.

### Background

There are approximately 3,000 new entrants in the schools in this Authority. Schools were consulted about the proposed urine study, aimed in order to obtain their co-operation.

In the week before the school medical was due to take place, the school nurse sent the parents a letter inviting them to participate in the urine study. The day before the school medical, the children were sent home with a bottle and another letter instructing parents how to obtain the early morning sample of urine. The children were then invited to bring the bottles to school to give to the school nurse, who then tested them, as soon as possible, using N-LABSTIX* reagent strips. The child's height was measured and blood pressure taken using standard techniques. In the schools where the staff and the school nurse were committed to the successful introduction of this programme, despite many fears on the part of both the school and school health staff, the results were most encouraging.

The trial has now been running since 1985 and results are reported from 1985–1989.

### Results

Results are presented according to the individual strip tests or combinations observed for these five-year-old girls and boys.

The findings for glucose in *Table 1* indicate a very low but equal incidence of glycosuria in both sexes – interestingly, both children with definite glycosuria also had "trace" ketonuria.

| Table 1 Distribution of Urine Strip Glucose Findings in Five-Year-Old Girls and Boys | | |

**Table 1**
**Distribution of Urine Strip Glucose Findings in Five-Year-Old Girls and Boys**

**Glucose Strip Result**

Girls:

| Negative | Trace | Positive (>28mmol/L) |
|---|---|---|
| 1566 (99.75%) | 3 (0.25%) | 1 |

Boys:

| Negative | Trace | Positive (>28mmol/L) |
|---|---|---|
| 1654 (99.76%) | 3 (0.24%) | 1 |

*There was 12.6% incidence of "Trace" proteinuria, and 1.6% of 0.3g/L or more*

There was again a very similar incidence of proteinuria in girls and boys (*Table 2*). However, 12.6% exhibited "trace" proteinuria and 1.6% had 0.3g/L or greater – including two children with 1g/L.

**Table 2**
**Distribution of Protein Strip Results in Girls and Boys**

**Protein Strip Result**

Girls:

| Negative | Trace | Positive |
|---|---|---|
| 1348 (85.7%) | 201 (12.7%) | 25 (1.6%) |

Boys:

| Negative | Trace | Positive |
|---|---|---|
| 1408 (85.9%) | 205 (12.5%) | 26 (1.6%) |

*Haematuria was more common in girls than in boys*

Haematuria was not very common (*Table 3*), although ten children demonstrated "small" or "moderate" amounts of blood. "Trace" included both haemolysed and non-haemolysed reactions. Haematuria was more common in girls.

| Table 3 | | |
|---|---|---|
| **Distribution of Blood Strip Results in Girls and Boys** | | |
| **Blood Strip Result** | | |
| **Girls:** | | |
| Negative | Trace | Positive |
| 1551 (98.7%) | 15 (0.95%) | 7 (0.45%) |
| **Boys:** | | |
| Negative | Trace | Positive |
| 1625 (99.3%) | 9 (0.55%) | 3 (0.18%) |

A positive Nitrite test was much more common in girls than in boys

Urinary tract infection, as implied by a positive Nitrite test, was much more prevalent in girls, occurring in 1.2% (*Table 4*). The urines from the two boys with a positive Nitrite test contained neither blood nor protein.

| Table 4 | |
|---|---|
| **Distribution of Nitrite Strip Results in Girls and Boys** | |
| **Nitrite Strip Result** | |
| **Girls:** | |
| Negative | Positive |
| 1527 (98.8%) | 18 (1.2%) |
| **Boys:** | |
| Negative | Positive |
| 1626 (99.9%) | 2 (0.1%) |

*Tables 5(a)* and *5(b)* show the combination of protein and blood strip results in girls and boys, respectively. Seven girls and two boys had "trace" or greater proteinuria and haematuria on initial testing, although only one girl had greater than "trace" for both blood and protein. This girl is currently being investigated. None of the "positive" proteinuric samples from boys contained any detectable blood.

## Table 5a
### Combination of Protein and Blood Strip Results in Girls

| Blood | Protein | | |
|---|---|---|---|
| | Negative | Trace | Positive |
| Negative | 1333 | 192† | 24 |
| Trace | 10 | 5 | 0 |
| Positive | 5 | 1 | 1 |

†One specimen was also Nitrite positive

## Table 5b
### Combination of Protein and Blood Strip Results in Boys

| Blood | Protein | | |
|---|---|---|---|
| | Negative | Trace | Positive |
| Negative | 1398 | 201 | 25 |
| Trace | 8 | 1 | 0 |
| Positive | 2 | 1 | 0 |

Of the eighteen girls with a positive Nitrite test, ten exhibited "trace" or greater proteinuria, one had a "trace" of blood, while two demonstrated ketonuria – presumably as the result of vomiting induced by infection. The two boys had no other strip abnormality.

## Table 6
### Combination of Positive Nitrite Tests with Other Strip Abnormalities in Girls

| | |
|---|---|
| Total Nitrite Positives | 18 |
| Trace Blood | 1 |
| Trace Protein | 6 |
| Positive Protein | 3 |
| Positive Blood + Positive Protein | 1 |
| Trace Ketones | 1 |
| Positive Ketones | 1 |
| No other abnormality | 5 |

## Discussion and Implications

Reagent strip analysis for the screening of paediatric urines has not been reported often. Boreland et al[1] report a false negative rate for UTI of 2.4% when looking at nitrite, blood and protein. Nitrite tests in particular exhibited a very high specificity and had a high predictive value for a negative result.

Proteinuria is commonly detected in childhood. The prevalence rate ranges from 5–6%, using a criterion of 0.3g/L. This study showed an incidence of 12.6% of urines containing "Trace" protein, and 1.6% showing 0.3g/L or more.

It should be noted that the level of proteinuria recorded on the reagent strip is greatly influenced by urinary concentration. Therefore, a "1+" reading from a dilute urine is more significant than a "1+" reading taken from urine with a high specific gravity or high osmolality, i.e. early morning.

This can be checked with the specific gravity reagent strip test. It may be that the difference in our results can be explained by the fact that these were early morning urines. However, it has been noted that for the initial reagent strip reading for proteinuria, the higher the initial result, the more likely it is that it will persist. Children presenting with 0.3g or 1g/L of proteinuria – even though asymptomatic – are more likely to have underlying renal disease to explain the finding.

*The higher the initial proteinuria reading, the more likely it is to persist*

*Children presenting with 0.3g/L or 1g/L of protein are more likely to have underlying renal disease.*

Routine screening studies in the past for asymptomatic proteinuria have failed to detect significant numbers of children with chronic renal disease. Wagner et al[2], in a study of 4,807 school children using a strip method for testing for proteinuria, found a prevalence of 5.4%. Randolph and Greenfield[3], utilising a strip method, reported a prevalence of proteinuria in pre-adolescent children of 6.3%. They also reported that it recurred in only 2.1%. Overall, the prevalence on one screening test was noted in 4.5% of boys by West[4] and in 6.4% of girls. In our study, 12.5% of urines contained a "trace", 1.6% contained 0.3g/L or more, and 0.6% of urines contained 1g/L or more.

*The detection rate for proteinuria was the same in boys and girls*

*Five-year-old children with any degree of proteinuria should at least be followed up at the 11-year-old school medical*

The overall detection rate for proteinuria was 7.0% in girls and 7.2% in boys. The commonest cause is probably benign proteinuria. Second specimens should be collected and then an assessment made on further evaluation, remembering that a very small number of these children will have an acute or chronic nephritis or urinary tract infection. In any event, they should be followed-up at the 11-year-old school medical with a further urine test.

The long-term benefits of the early detection of proteinuria and haematuria are now becoming clear, along the lines discussed some years ago by Dodge et al[5].

The widely used Ames urine testing strip for blood records the presence of blood in the urine as "non-haemolysed trace", "haemolysed trace", "small", "moderate", or "large" amounts. In the experience of Norman[6,7], a reading of "non-haemolysed trace" may be associated with less than 5–10 red blood cells per high power field on a freshly voided specimen.

That asymptomatic micro-haematuria in children is common, is questioned. Several large cross-sectional screening studies of school-age children have estimated an incidence of 0.1% to 0.5%. In our study, the incidence was approximately 1%, but if one excludes haemolysed and non-haemolysed traces, the incidence was 6 out of 3,260 urines. However, "trace" haematuria may be clinically significant, especially if the observation can be repeated[8].

The main diagnoses to consider are urinary tract infection, benign recurrent or persistent haematuria, trauma, or acute or chronic nephritis of various types.

In Norman's experience, the commonest diagnosis was benign recurrent or persistent haematuria. However, in some other studies idiopathic hypocalciuria has also been found to occur.

*Gross and asymptomatic micro-haematuria should be investigated.*

Indications for diagnostic investigation are:

1. Episodes of gross as well as microscopic haematuria

2. The presence of proteinuria or infection in the urine

3. Parental anxiety.

Looking for asymptomatic bacteriuria, 0.6% of the samples were found to have a positive nitrite test indicative of infection; of these, eight also contained protein and one contained blood. The incidence of asymptomatic bacteriuria is much less than in other recorded studies. Follow-up on children with abnormal findings consisted of further MSU's and on some occasions IVU. We would agree with the Guy's approach on renal failure, that if every child in Britain with a urinary tract infection were diagnosed and properly investigated and treated, this cause of renal failure might be eradicated.

*Diagnosis of every case of UTI in children could lead to the eradication of this cause of renal failure.*

Eight urines (0.25%) contained glucose, and obviously these children are being checked for diabetes mellitus.

A positive outcome from urine screening in young children remains unknown at present. This is not unexpected, since current knowledge of the long-term progression of these children is not yet known. Therefore, bearing in mind the encouraging results we have observed, long-term studies are recommended to define the outcome.

## Conclusions

The study has shown that it is feasible to set up a urine screening programme in schools, run by nurses.

The preliminary results from the study indicate that significant numbers of children were picked up with protein, blood, glucose or evidence of infection in the urine, and this certainly merits further study.

Both short and long-term studies need to be completed on this population before any definite comments can be made as to the cost-effectiveness of such a screening programme in terms of identification and prevention of long-term chronic disease. However, the cost and hardships of waiting for advanced disease to manifest in later life must be a major consideration.

## References

1. Boreland, P.C., Stoker, M. Dipstick analysis for screening of paediatric urine. J.Clin.Pathol. (1986); **39**: 1360–1362.

2. Wagner, M.G., Smith, F.G., et al. Epidemiology of proteinuria. J.Pediatr. (1968); **73** (6): 825–832.

3. Randolph, M.F., Greenfield, M., Proteinuria: a 6-year study of normal infants, pre-school and school-age populations previously screened for urinary tract disease. Am.J.Dis.Child. (1967); **114**: 631–638.

4. West, C.D., Medical Progress. Asymptomatic proteinuria and haematuria in children. J.Pediatr. (1976); **89**: 173–182.

5.  Dodge, W.F., West, E.F., et al. Proteinuria and haematuria in schoolchildren. Epidemiology and early natural history. J.Pediatr. (1976); **88** (2): 327–347.

6.  Norman, M.E., Office approach to haematuria and proteinuria. Ped.Clinics of N.America (1987); **34** (3): 545–560.

7.  Norman, M.E., Asymptomatic proteinuria and haematuria in children. Delaware Med.J. (1983); **55** (5): 271–277.

8.  Arm, J.P., Peile, E.G., Rainford, D.J., Significance of dipstick haematuria. 2. Correlation with pathology. Brit.J.Urol. (1986); **58**: 218–223.

# Urinalysis in the Antenatal Setting

**Dr J.B. Scrimgeour**
Consultant & Senior Lecturer,
Western General Hospital, Edinburgh

While pregnant patients may be regarded as an ideal population to screen for various asymptomatic disorders, it is essential that consideration be given to screening *prior* to a pregnancy – thus allowing any positive result to be fully investigated and treated. This screening may be carried out in a formal Pre-Conception Clinic at hospitals, but generally patients referred to such a clinic have a known disorder, already treated but for whom pregnancy may have implications, potentially putting the mother and/or the baby at risk. For the majority of the female population, I firmly believe that each visit to a Family Planning Clinic should be overtly regarded by the practitioners and nurses as a "pre-pregnancy" clinic, and the opportunity taken at those visits to ensure that, should the patients stop their current contraceptive method, they will be fit for the ensuing pregnancy.

At each antenatal visit, whether to hospital or to the general practice, patients are requested to bring a specimen of urine for testing. At the first visit a general screen of the urine is necessary, but at subsequent visits, assuming the initial screen to be negative, tests may be limited to ketonuria, glycosuria, proteinuria and bacteriuria. Of these, proteinuria is the most important, as it may indicate the development of moderately severe pre-eclampsia, which in turn can have a disastrous outcome for both mother and child.

### The Prevalence of Conditions Associated with Abnormal Reagent Strip Test Results

#### Ketonuria

Nausea and vomiting are extremely common in early pregnancy, but are usually alleviated by small frequent feeds, fluids and, if necessary, anti-emetics. Where such treatment is not effective, the vomiting may be persistent to the extent that the patient loses weight, and becomes dehydrated and ketotic. Often it is the ketosis – detected on routine screening – which indicates the severity of the condition, as a baseline weight is often unknown for an individual patient and dehydration is not easy to diagnose unless severe. However, an assessment of the state of dehydration can now be made by measuring the urine specific gravity with a reagent strip test. This severe vomiting during early pregnancy is known as hyperemesis gravidarum, requires hospital admission, and occurs in about 0.5% of patients.

Do remember, however, that you may also have a previously undiagnosed diabetic on your hands with diabetic ketoacidosis!

#### Glycosuria

Glycosuria during pregnancy is extremely common, and is usually attributed to a lowered renal threshold for glucose during pregnancy. This conclusion can only be reached, however, after a glucose tolerance test has been performed to exclude diabetes mellitus. In a series reported from Newport, Monmouthshire, over 9% of 1500 patients showed glycosuria at some point during their pregnancy.

## Table 1
## At-Risk Factors for Diabetes in Pregnancy

- Weight greater than 120% of standard weight for height
- Affected sibling, parent or grandparent
- Previous baby greater than 4.5Kg (10lbs) at birth
- Previous unexplained stillbirth
- Two or more spontaneous abortions
- Glycosuria on *second* urine specimen collected before breakfast on two or more occasions

In screening patients for overt or even gestational diabetes (also called covert diabetes), the history of the patient must be reviewed and account taken of the urine result.

Certain risk factors for diabetes must be considered. These include over-weight, affected relative, previous high birth-weight baby, previous unexplained stillbirth or spontaneous abortions, or glycosuria on the *second* urine specimen before breakfast (*Table 1*). Having identified these risk factors, immediate practical management includes a fasting blood glucose estimation or a glucose tolerance test, as outlined in *Table 2*.

## Table 2
## Immediate Management of Patients with Diabetes Risk Factors

| Risk | Follow-Up Test |
|---|---|
| Glycosuria | Fasting blood glucose |
| One or more at-risk factors excluding glycosuria | Fasting blood glucose |
| Glycosuria and one or more risk factors | Glucose tolerance test |
| Fasting plasma glucose at less than 32 weeks gestation >5.5mmol/L | Glucose tolerance test |
| Fasting plasma glucose at more than 32 weeks gestation >6mmol/L | Glucose tolerance test |

### Proteinuria

Increasing proteinuria is a poor prognostic sign in pre-eclampsia

Proteinuria should be tested for at each antenatal attendance. Increasing proteinuria is a poor prognostic sign in pre-eclampsia, and must therefore be thoroughly investigated. It is generally agreed that the maximum daily excretion of protein should not exceed 300mg, while in single specimens, concentrations more than 0.3g per litre ("1+" on ALBUSTIX*) are considered significant if found in two or more random specimens collected at least six hours apart; less than this may be the result of contamination.

A single positive protein strip test result on a random sample may also indicate contamination by vaginal discharge or bleeding per vagina; urinary tract infection; or orthostatic (postural) proteinuria – which occurs in 5–20% of young adults (*Table 3*). In these circumstances a clean, mid-stream urine specimen should be sent for full bacteriological culture and examination.

| Table 3 |
| Causes of Proteinura in a Random Urine Sample |

- Pre-eclampsia
- Contamination by vaginal discharge
- Contamination by bleeding per vagina
- Urinary tract infection
- Orthostatic (postural) proteinuria

### Bacteriuria

In the middle trimester,
UTI is the commonest
complication of
pregnancy

Bacteriuria is more common during pregnancy, and urinary tract infection is the commonest complication of pregnancy in the middle trimester. Asymptomatic bacteriuria must be tested for at the initial pregnancy consultation. This can be performed either by reagent strip testing for nitrite, together with leucocytes, protein and blood, or by a formal mid-stream specimen of urine. It has been shown in various series that up to 7% of pregnant patients have asymptomatic bacteriuria, and 7% of those have identifiable renal pathology. This means that if the screening is carried out efficiently, then those patients with pathology can have preliminary investigations carried out during the pregnancy, and more detailed investigations after the pregnancy.

Those patients found to have asymptomatic bacteriuria on two successive occasions should have appropriate antibiotic therapy to clear the urinary tract infection. If this is not done, then the patient runs the risk of a full-blown urinary tract infection and fluctuant pyrexia, which may in turn precipitate premature labour.

### Why Test Urine in Pregnancy?

The patient who is pregnant for the first time may not have visited her general practitioner for many years – possibly the last time was when she was vaccinated! Pregnancy, and especially at the booking visit, is an opportunity which must not be missed to review the patient's whole health and social status. In such a review it is very simple to test the urine using reagent strip tests, and use this as a screen for many disorders. Particular attention should be paid to proteinuria, glycosuria, ketonuria and bacteriuria, but at the first visit the full N-MULTISTIX* SG or MULTISTIX* 10SG screen is justified.

Subsequent visits to the antenatal clinic and the detail of the urine testing will depend on the results from the first consultation; however, in the first trimester ketonuria must be excluded, while throughout the pregnancy proteinuria and glycosuria must be excluded.

### The Clinical Significance of Abnormal Results

Having found a positive result on testing the urine, it is essential that the appropriate subsequent investigation is known and instituted.

While hyperemesis gravidarum is the likely diagnosis, the question must also be posed as to why should *this* patient have hyperemesis and not the other ten patients at the clinic today. As stated above, the ketonuria may not be directly related to the pregnancy but may be her first episode of diabetic ketoacidosis. Admission to hospital is necessary immediately after initial resuscitative measures have been taken. The ketonuria may also be due to simple · dehydration following a bout of self-imposed starvation, or to gastro-enteritis. Ensure that it is not appendicitis, which is notoriously difficult to diagnose during pregnancy.

Ketonuria may be the first sign to indicate an abnormality of the pregnancy itself, in the form of hydatidiform mole or a multiple pregnancy. An ultrasound examination would clarify this situation. These factors are summarised in *Table 4.*

Ketonuria may indicate the first episode of ketoacidosis. This necessitates hospital admission

| Table 4 |
| --- |
| **Causes of Ketonuria in Pregnancy** |
| • Hyperemesis gravidarum |
| • Diabetic ketoacidosis |
| • Starvation – induced dehydration |
| • Gastro-enteritis |
| • Appendicitis |
| • Hydatidiform mole |
| • Multiple pregnancy |

*Glycosuria*

As previously mentioned, glycosuria may be the first indication of gestational diabetes. Further enquiry may be necessary to find out about affected relatives or previous pregnancies. I find that the commonest "cause" of glycosuria is simply that the patient has brought along any conveniently timed specimen of urine – usually having forgotten until she is about to leave home. The *second* fasting specimen is therefore to be emphasised before embarking on further investigation such as a glucose tolerance test, so that the effects of the previous evening meal may be excluded.

Gestational diabetes should be confirmed. Follow-up may prevent subsequent foetal malformation

Should gestational diabetes be confirmed, then she should be followed up at a combined antenatal/diabetic hospital clinic by an interested obstetrician and diabetologist. Only in this way will diet or insulin be controlled effectively, and macrosomic babies avoided with their increased incidence of foetal malformation.

*Proteinuria*

Hypertension and proteinuria have a dramatic effect on the perinatal death rate

Exclusion of the other causes of proteinuria, as indicated above, will leave the outstanding possibility of pre-eclampsia as the cause. The significance of this finding cannot be underestimated. The effect of hypertension and/or proteinuria on the stillbirth and deaths in the first week of life (Perinatal Death Rate) is dramatic, and is illustrated in *Table 5.*

| Table 5 Effects of Hypertension and Proteinuria on the Perinatal Death Rate | |
| --- | --- |
| **Group** | **Perinatal Death Rate /1000 Births** |
| Normal | 10 |
| Hypertension only | 26 |
| Hypertension plus proteinuria | 37.9 |

If the patient is known to be hypertensive prior to the pregnancy, this finding hopefully should have already been fully investigated and treatment instituted. If hypertension and proteinuria develop during pregnancy, refer the patient to the hospital immediately. Do *not* procrastinate – this phenomenon is a prelude to eclampsia, which in turn can be fatal for both mother and child if ignored.

### Bacteriuria

Once contamination of the original specimen has been excluded and a repeat MSU confirms the finding, antibiotic therapy is indicated.

Further investigation after the pregnancy is over will be required to exclude urinary pathology. However, remember that it takes around eight weeks after delivery before the hormonal and pressure effects of the pregnancy on the urinary tract have resolved.

### Where Should Testing Be Performed?

Simply, wherever and whenever an antenatal patient is being examined. That may be in the General Practitioner's surgery, the patient's home, the hospital antenatal clinic or the hospital ward. Be sure, however, if you are not doing the test yourself, that the nurse or colleague records the result and makes any abnormal finding known. Too often, abnormal results are recorded but no action is taken to confirm or investigate them.

### Practical Problems During Testing in Pregnancy

The most obvious problem is that of reminding the patient to bring the specimen. Initially, the specimen may arrive in a variety of shapes and sizes of containers, many of which may have been inadequately cleaned and therefore liable to give false results. It is preferable to provide the patient with a clean universal container for subsequent specimens.

Some patients find it difficult to believe we actually do need the second specimen of urine prior to breakfast, but when it is explained that we do not want the specimen which has been lying in the bladder overnight but the one prior to her breakfast, she usually sees the light.

Contamination, usually by vaginal discharge, is common. If it is thought to be the cause of "proteinuria", then this can be circumvented by asking the nurse to supervise the patient during the taking of the mid-stream specimen of urine.

Any positive reagent
strip results must be
reported to the person in
charge of the clinic

Finally, emphasis must again be made of the importance of any positive results being reported to the person in charge of the clinic, so that the patient can be further investigated if necessary.

### Benefits of Urinalysis During Pregnancy

The entire object of screening urine specimens during pregnancy is to diagnose existing disorders, or to monitor progress or the effect of treatment. The earlier the diagnosis is made, the sooner treatment can be started – to the immediate benefit of both mother and child.

### The Future

A specimen of urine is such an easy sample to obtain that its value must be maximised. Screening is increasingly used to detect disorders before they become clinically obvious, and urine abnormalities require further investigation to identify other disorders.

Inevitably, the cost-effectiveness of such screening must be known, and while it may not be cost-effective in some disorders to screen the entire population, it may be that by using selective criteria, those most liable to the disorder under investigation could be screened and effectively counselled.

# The Rapid Diagnosis of Urinary Tract Infection in the Hospital and Community: Reagent Strip Testing

## Dr. N. F. Lightfoot
Director, Public Health Laboratory, Newcastle upon Tyne

Previously Director, Public Health Laboratory, Taunton, Somerset

## INTRODUCTION

UTI's are the commonest condition for prescribing antibiotics

Only half the women presenting to their GP's with symptoms have significant infection

The patient deserves an instant answer to the cause of the symptoms

Urinary tract infections are the commonest condition for which a general practitioner prescribes an antibiotic[1], and make up 2% of the consultation workload. Most of them are uncomplicated and are caused by common species of bacteria that make up the normal flora of the perineum. Fastidious organisms such as *Lactobacillus* and *Chlamydia trachomatis* have been discovered as less common causes. Only half the women presenting to their General Practitioners with symptoms have been found to have significant infection. Some of these patients with culture-negative urines have the urethral syndrome, and in others the symptoms may be due to psycho-physiological reactions or chemical irritation. The patient deserves an instant answer to the cause of the symptoms and presents a dilemma to the doctor in decision-making: the severity of the symptoms do not accurately predict a treatable cause, and the traditional laboratory investigation may take 48 hours or longer. There is a need for rapid diagnostic methods to improve patient care.

## PATHOGENESIS

Micro-organisms gain access to the bladder following meatal colonisation and ascend the urethra; they adhere to the bladder urothelium and produce inflammatory changes. Complications such as pyelonephritis do not commonly ensue, but anatomical abnormalities predispose to ascending infection. The inflammatory changes in the urethra and bladder produce the well recognised symptoms of dysuria, frequency, nocturia and suprapubic pain.

Some patients present with symptoms but have no identifiable infection when investigated.

Occasionally haematuria and fever occur. Antibiotic therapy in uncomplicated urinary tract infection is nearly always effective, and in general practice it is not always necessary to know the antibiotic sensitivities of the infecting organism. Some patients, however, present with many of the symptoms and yet have no identifiable infection when investigated. The effect of antibiotic treatment on this group of patients has not been properly investigated, and there is yet another group of patients whose symptoms resolve without medical intervention. The measurement of bacterial invasion and the inflammatory changes produced provide a method for the diagnosis of urinary tract infection and the initiation of treatment.

## DIAGNOSIS

The traditional laboratory diagnosis may take 48 hours or more

The clinical diagnosis of uncomplicated urinary tract infection is imprecise; symptoms and signs have been shown to be inaccurate predictors of infection[2], even when culture for fastidious organisms has been included[3]. The traditional laboratory diagnosis of measuring white cells by microscopy and semi-quantitative culture of bacteria may take 48 hours or more when the time to collect and transport the specimen, the time for the laboratory examination and the transit time of the report are taken into account.

The estimation of the numbers of bacteria present in a mid-stream specimen of urine is influenced by several factors, particularly the care in collection and its time in transit to the examining laboratory. There are always small numbers of bacteria present in mid-stream urine specimens; the significant number has usually been taken to be $10^8$ organisms per litre based on the original investigations of Kass[4]. More recently, we have taken lower threshold limits of $10^7$ organisms per litre, particularly for Gram positive organisms, and it has been suggested that bacterial counts should be interpreted individually for each patient.

The rapid measurement of other less direct indications of bacterial invasion should therefore be considered.

## RAPID METHODS

### a) In the Laboratory

Several methods have been described for the detection of bacteria in urine. These include changes in electrical impedance[5], measurement of bacterial adenosine triphosphate by luciferase[6], fluorescence staining and acridine orange staining[7], and particle counting[8]. These methods are appropriate for use in laboratories, and give excellent predictive values for a negative result (97% – 100%); however, they do not predict a positive result with sufficient accuracy to commence antibiotic treatment. They can be used to screen out specimens needing no further investigation.

Microscopy provides a rapid, inexpensive screening test, but the false positive rate is high as leucocytes are often found in excessive numbers in uninfected patients. Leucocytes may also be absent in patients with urinary tract infection.

These tests are laboratory-based and can significantly decrease the investigation time for negative specimens.

### b) At the Patient's Side

There are methods for examining urine that do not require complicated equipment and can be performed at the patient interview. Nitrite, blood, protein and leucocyte esterase can be measured using a reagent strip test, and a visual assessment of turbidity can be made.

| Table 1 Rapid Tests for Urinary Tract Infection at the Patient's Side |
| --- |
| • Symptoms |
| • Nitrite |
| • Protein |
| • Blood |
| • Leucocytes |
| • Specimen Appearance |

### Nitrite

Many species of bacteria that infect the urinary tract can metabolise dietary nitrate excreted in the urine to nitrite. The detection of nitrite in urine is therefore a valuable indicator of the extent of bacterial invasion of the bladder. The amount of nitrite produced is influenced by the time the invading bacteria have been incubated in bladder urine, and should be at least three hours. The original method of Greiss[10] used liquid reagents, but this cumbersome method has been replaced by a reagent strip test. The strip is impregnated with p-arsanilic acid and tetrahydrobenzo (h)quinoline-3-ol, and turns pink when exposed to nitrite. The reagent strip is dipped into freshly passed urine, removed and held against a white background; a pink colour indicates a positive result. False positive results are not encountered; false negative results may occur if the bacteria do not metabolise nitrate, or if the bacteria have not been incubated for a long enough period in the urine. Boric acid preservative does not affect the performance of the test.

### Protein and Blood

Proteinuria and haematuria may follow bacterial invasion of the bladder mucosa, and can also be detected in urine by reagent strip tests. There are, however, other non-infective causes of proteinuria and haematuria, reducing the specificity of these tests. Haematuria is an infrequent finding in uncomplicated urinary tract infection, and in isolation reduces the diagnostic sensitivity.

### Leucocyte esterase

White cells are normally found in urine, but an increase (pyuria) is an indication of inflammatory changes. Leucocyte esterase measurement has been shown to accurately reflect the numbers of leucocytes present[11]. Not all bacterial infections of the lower urinary tract are accompanied by pyuria, and pyuria may often be present in non-infective conditions.

### Turbidity

Infected urines are often turbid on naked eye examination, but there are other non-infective causes of turbid urines – such as the presence of phosphate – giving rise to false positive results. Clear urines are not usually infected.

### Combined tests

Each of these tests when used alone have relatively poor sensitivity and specificity – other than the specificity for nitrite – and cannot be relied upon to accurately predict urinary tract infection in random samples. When the tests are *combined*, the sensitivity increases from 57.4% (nitrite test alone) through 90.1% (nitrite and appearance together) to 96.9% (nitrite, blood, protein and appearance positive in any combination), whereas the specificity decreases from 99.5% to 48.9%[12]. The predictive value for negative tests increases as more parameters are considered, while those for a positive test show the reverse trend. The combined tests, all parameters being negative, can therefore be used confidently to identify uninfected urines that do not merit any further investigation. The very small number of patients with true infections and negative rapid tests can be protected by asking the patients to return if the symptoms persist at 48 hours. It is estimated that a typical GP will see such a patient returning with symptoms after 48 hours once every three years.

The combined strip tests can be confidently used to identify uninfected urines

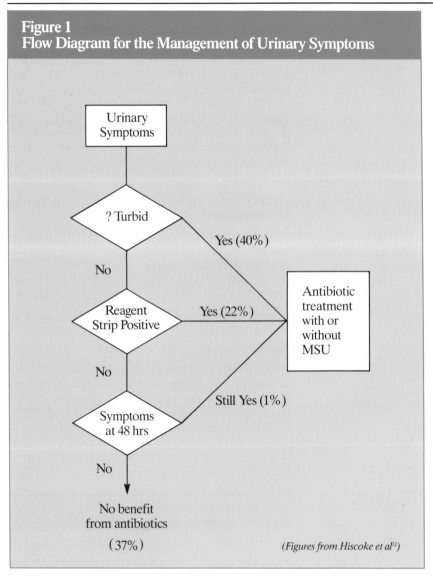

**Figure 1**
**Flow Diagram for the Management of Urinary Symptoms**

Urinary Symptoms

? Turbid — Yes (40%)

No

Reagent Strip Positive — Yes (22%)

No

Symptoms at 48 hrs — Still Yes (1%)

No

Antibiotic treatment with or without MSU

No benefit from antibiotics (37%)

*(Figures from Hiscoke et al[12])*

## CLINICAL DECISION MAKING

*If all rapid tests are negative, antibiotic treatment can be withheld, even in the presence of symptoms*

When a patient presents to her general practitioner, the rapid reagent strip tests can be performed at the patient interview, and if all are negative antibiotic treatment can be withheld with confidence, even in the presence of symptoms. Positive results indicate that treatment may be appropriate and further laboratory investigations may be required. The advantages of this approach are quite considerable; the laboratory workload will be decreased by 30–40%[13], and patients are not given unnecessary antibiotics. This is important in minimising the side-effects of antibiotic therapy and preventing the emergence of resistant bacteria.

*The laboratory workload will decrease by 30–40%*

These tests are advocated for use in patients presenting with uncomplicated urinary tract infections. They make up the greatest proportion of patients presenting with symptoms, but patients presenting with repeated or recurrent infections should usually be investigated by routine laboratory methods – although the rapid tests may give early information on which to base treatment that will later be confirmed. Infections in children or pregnant women should usually be confirmed by laboratory culture.

Reagent strip tests are considerably less expensive than laboratory tests

The cost of reagent strip urine analysis is about £0.15, and is considerably cheaper than the laboratory costs which are estimated to be about £10. It improves patient care by its rapidity, reduces the exposure to unnecessary antibiotics and reduces the laboratory costs. Perhaps it is what is expected of us during the present debate about the effectiveness of present patient care systems.

### References

1. Brooks, D., Mallick, N. Renal Medicine and Urology, Edinburgh: Churchill Livingstone (1982), 56–97.

2. Moud, N.C., Percival, A., Williams, J.D., Brumfitt, W. Presentation, diagnosis and treatment of urinary tract infections in General Practice. Lancet (1965); 1: 514–516.

3. Smith, K, Lightfoot, N.F., Greig, D., Yoxall, M., Ewings, P. Clinical judgement alone is no longer appropriate in the diagnosis of bacterial urinary tract infection in women in General Practice. Submitted for publication.

4. Kass, E.H. Bacteriuria and the diagnosis of infections in the urinary tract. Archives of Internal Medicine (1951); 100: 709–714.

5. Cady, P., Dufour, S.W., Lawless, P., Nunke, B. Impedimetric screening for bacteriuria. J.Clin.Microbiol. (1978); 7: 273–278.

6. Schifman, R.B., Weiden, M., Brooker, J. Bacteriuria screening by direct bioluminescence assay of ATP. J.Clin.Microbiol. (1948); 20: 644–648.

7. Scholefield, J., Manson, R., Johnston, R.T., Scott, R. The use of acridine-orange staining in image analysis to detect bacteriuria. Urol.Res. (1985); 13: 141–142.

8. Dow, C.S., France, A.D., Khan, M.S., Johnson, T. Particle size distribution analysis for the rapid detection of microbial infection in urine. J.Clin.Pathol. (1979); 32: 386–390.

9. Smith, T.K., Hudson, Andrea, J., Spencer, R.C. Evaluation of six screening methods for detecting significant bacteriuria. J.Clin.Pathol., (1988); 41: 904–909.

10. Schaus, R. Greiss' Nitrate Test in the diagnosis of urinary tract infection. J.Am.Med.Assoc. (1956); 161: 528.

11. Herliky, R.E., Wilkensen, R., Roy, J.B. New and rapid method for detection of pyuria by leucocyte esterase reaction. Urology (1984); 23: 148–149.

12. Hiscoke, C., Yoxall, M., Greig, D., Lightfoot, N.F. A Validation of the rapid diagnosis of urinary tract infection in routine microbiology laboratories and in General Practice. Submitted for Publication.

13. Harrogan, P.G., Rooney, P.G., Dawes, E.A., Stout, R.W. Evaluation of four screening tests for bacteriuria in elderly people. Lancet (1989); 1: 1117–1119.

# Urinary Tract Infection in the Elderly

**Dr. P. J. Evans**
Department of General and Geriatric Medicine
Guy's Hospital, London
Current post: Consultant Physician/Hon. Senior Lecturer
Ealing and Hammersmith Hospitals, London

*At least 20% of women and 10% of men over 65 have significant bacteriuria*

There is a marked increase in the prevalence of chronic urinary tract infection (UTI) in both sexes with advancing age. At least 20% of women and 10% of men over 65 years of age have significant bacteriuria[4,6,12]. The prevalence of infection is greatest in long-stay geriatric patients and least in elderly patients living at home[2,6,14,18]. Elderly patients living in residential homes appear to come midway in the ranking[7].

*The majority of elderly subjects with bacteriuria do not have symptoms of UTI and may present atypically*

The majority of elderly subjects with bacteriuria do not have symptoms of urinary tract infection[4]. In addition, elderly patients with bacteriuria are frequently apyrexial and have normal peripheral white blood cell counts (personal observations). These factors combine to make the diagnosis of urinary tract infection very difficult.

Three groups of elderly patients with bacteriuria can be identified (*Table 1*). These are:

1. Patients with classical symptoms of urinary tract infection, i.e, dysuria, frequency and haematuria.
2. Patients who are asymptomatic, i.e. the majority.
3. Patients presenting atypically with a history of falls, immobility, confusion and general poor health.

Patients in group one pose little problem and can be treated without delay. Patients in group two probably do not need treating, as there is substantial evidence to suggest that asymptomatic bacteriuria in the elderly does not affect patient survival[10,15]. This view is not universally held, however[8,9,17].

Patients in group three are usually admitted to hospital for further investigation. An important part of the inpatient workup will include a search for sepsis. Specimens sent for culture will include a mid-stream specimen of urine (MSU), sputum and possibly blood. It is in this group of patients that reagent strip testing of urine for infection has its greatest value, by providing an almost immediate result. Effective treatment of infection in these patients will lead to recovery and possibly earlier discharge in many cases (see *Figure 1*).

*Effective treatment of infection will lead to recovery in many cases*

| Table 1 Characteristics of Elderly Patients with Urinary Tract Infection | |
| --- | --- |
| **Classical Symptoms of UTI** | Dysuria Frequency Haematuria |
| **Atypical Symptoms** | Falls Immobility Confusion General poor health |

### Pre-disposing Factors for Urinary Tract Infection in the Elderly

Inadequate flushing of the bladder, either due to reduced fluid intake or reduced thirst sensation, increases the risk of urinary infection in the elderly. Inadequate bladder emptying leading to an increased residual volume is also a major predisposing factor for infection[16]. Causes include immobility, drugs (especially diuretics, tricyclic antidepressants and some antiarrhythmics), abnormal bladder control (for example after a cerebrovascular accident) and bladder outlet obstruction (for example, secondary to an enlarged prostate). Faecal impaction increases the risk of urinary infection in two ways. Firstly, it may cause faecal soiling and contamination of the perineum and, secondly, it can lead to incomplete bladder emptying and stagnation of urine. Finally, instrumentation and catheterisation of the urinary tract are performed more commonly in the elderly and carry an increased risk of bladder infection. These factors are summarised in *Table 2*.

---

**Table 2**
**Main Pre-disposing Factors for UTI in the Elderly**

1. **Reduced flushing of the bladder**

2. **Increased stagnation of urine**
   (a) Immobility
   (b) Urinary retention

3. **Catheterisation/instrumentation of urinary tract**

4. **Faecal impaction/incontinence**

---

### Laboratory Investigation of Urinary Tract Infections in the Elderly

#### 1. Microscopy

Pyuria is considered to be a marker of urinary tract infection, and is defined as $>10$ leucocytes/$\mu$l of uncentrifuged urine. In the elderly, pyuria is common even in the absence of bacteriuria, and is therefore a poor predictor of infection[1]. However, the presence of pyuria without bacteriuria still has considerable clinical importance and should not be ignored in elderly patients.

*The presence of pyuria without bacteriuria has considerable clinical importance in elderly patients*

#### 2. Mid-stream Specimen of Urine (MSU)

Urine samples are difficult to collect from elderly patients – especially immobile women where the contamination rate is high. Impaired voluntary control of micturition adds to the difficulties encountered in obtaining adequate urine samples. Suprapubic aspiration is usually not very helpful, because many elderly patients cannot retain enough urine to make the bladder palpable above the symphysis pubis. In cases of extreme difficulty, an aseptic diagnostic catheterisation is justified.

The diagnosis of urinary tract infection is made on the basis of a bacterial count of $>10^5$ organisms/ml of urine[11], although some workers feel that this criterion cannot now be applied universally[13]. A single mid-stream specimen of urine has an accuracy of 80%. This accuracy increases to 95% with two consecutive urine samples, and to 97% with three consecutive urine samples[3].

### 3. Reagent Strip Testing

In a study of fifty consecutive admissions to the geriatric department, each patient provided a mid-stream specimen of urine. One half was sent for standard microscopy and culture and the other half reagent strip tested for nitrite, blood, protein greater than "1+" using N-LABSTIX* reagent strips and urinary leucocyte count >10/μl. The results of this study, demonstrating the sensitivity and specificity of nitrite, blood, protein and urinary leucocytes in the detection of urinary infection, are shown in *Table 3*.

| Table 3 Reagent Strip Test Results for Elderly Hospital In-Patients | | |
|---|---|---|
| (N=50) | Sensitivity (%) | Specificity (%) |
| Nitrite | 83 | 100 |
| Blood | 67 | 83 |
| Protein | 72 | 87 |
| Urinary leucocytes | 72 | 87 |

Nitrite was the most accurate indicator of UTI, and can be reliably used for early detection in acutely ill elderly patients

Combination strip testing for nitrite, blood and protein was 100% reliable for detecting UTI

These data show that urinary nitrite was the most accurate indicator of urinary tract infections in the elderly, with 83% of infections being detected on admission. Further, all urines with a positive nitrite were MSU culture positive. Urinary nitrite can therefore be reliably used for the early detection of urinary tract infections in acutely ill elderly patients.

If one or more of the strip test results for nitrite, blood or protein were positive, then all cases of infection were identified, i.e. combination strip testing for nitrite, blood and protein was 100% reliable for detecting urinary tract infection.

### 4. Protocol for the Detection and Management of Urinary Tract Infection in Elderly Patients Presenting Atypically.

A suggested outline protocol for this group of patients is presented in *Figure 1*.

### Conclusions

In conclusion, asymptomatic bacteriuria is common in the elderly. Elderly patients with urinary tract infections may present atypically with falls, confusion, immobility and generally poor health. The diagnosis of urinary infection on admission of these patients is facilitated by the use of reagent strip testing of urine, especially for nitrite. This will allow treatment to be started earlier, whilst awaiting the results from urine culture and sensitivity. With the increasing numbers of elderly patients in society, a quick and reliable method for the early detection of urinary infection is essential.

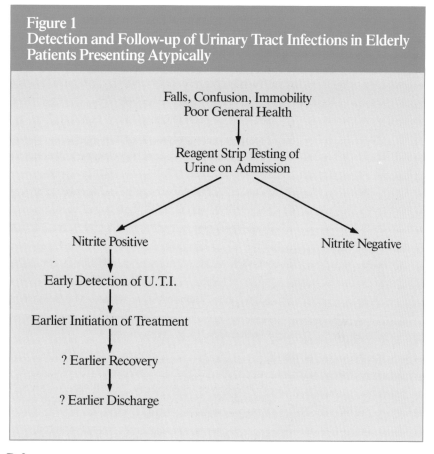

**Figure 1**
**Detection and Follow-up of Urinary Tract Infections in Elderly Patients Presenting Atypically**

Falls, Confusion, Immobility
Poor General Health

Reagent Strip Testing of
Urine on Admission

Nitrite Positive

Nitrite Negative

Early Detection of U.T.I.

Earlier Initiation of Treatment

? Earlier Recovery

? Earlier Discharge

**References**

1. Abrutyn, E., Boscia, J.A. and Kaye, D. The treatment of asymptomatic bacteriuria in the elderly. J.Am.Geriatr.Soc. (1988); **36**: 473–475.

2. Ahktar, H.R., Andrews, G.R., Caird, F.I. and Fallon, R.J. Urinary tract infection in the elderly: A population study. Age and Ageing (1972); **1**: 48–54.

3. Andriole, V.T. in: Urinary tract infection and its management. Ed: D. Kaye. P 37 St. Louis, USA: C.I. Mosby Co. (1972).

4. Boscia, J.A., Kobasa, W.D., Arbutyn, E., Levison, M.E., Kaplan, A.M. and Kaye, D. Lack of association between bacteriuria and symptoms in the elderly. Am.J.Med. (1986); **81**: 979–82.

5. Boscia, J.A., Kobasa, W.D., Knight, R.A., Abrutyn, E., Levison, M.E. and Kaye, D. Epidemiology of bacteriuria in an elderly ambulatory population. Am.J.Med. (1986); **80**: 208–214.

6. Brocklehurst, J.C., Dillane, J.B., Griffiths, L. and Fry, J. The prevalence and symptomatology of urinary infection in an aged population. Gerontol.Clin. (1968); **10**: 242–253.

7. Dontas, A.S., Papanayiotou, P.C. and Papanicolaou, N.T. The effect of bacteriuria on renal function patterns of old age. Clin.Sci. (1968); **34**: 73–81.

8. Dontas, A.S., Kasviki-Charvatai, P. Papanayiotou, P.C. and Marketos, S.G. Bacteriuria and survival in old age. New Eng.J.Med. (1981); **305**: 939–43.

9. Evans, D.A., Kass, E.H., Hennekens, C.H., et al. Bacteriuria and subsequent mortality in women. Lancet (1982); **1**: 156–8.

10. Heinamaki, P., Haavisto, S.M., Hakulinen, T., Uattila, K., Rajala, S. Mortality in relation to urinary characteristics in the very aged. Gerontology (1986); **32**: 167–171.

11. Kass, E.H. Bacteriuria and the diagnosis of infections of the urinary tract. Arch.Int.Med. (1957); **100**: 709–713.

12. Kasviki-Charvati, P., Drolette-Kefakis, B., Papanayiotou, P.C. et al. Turnover of bacteriuria in old age. Age and Ageing (1982); **11**: 169.

13. Maskell, R. in: Urinary tract infection in clinical and laboratory practice. First Edition 1988. Edward Arnold, London. Chapter 2, p36.

14. Milne, J.S., Williamson, J., Maule, M.M. and Wallace, T. Urinary symptoms in older people. Mod.Geriatr. (1972); **2**: 198–213.

15. Nordenstam, G.R., Brandberg, C.A., Oden, A.S., Svanborg-Eden, C.M. and Svanborg, A. Bacteriuria and mortality in an elderly population. New Eng.J.Med. (1986); **314**: 1152–1156.

16. Shand, D.G., O'Grady, F., Nimmon, C.C. and Cattell, W.R. Relation between residual urine volume and response to treatment of urinary infection. Lancet (1970); **1**: 1305–6.

17. Sourander, L.B. Urinary tract infection in the aged: Epidemiological Study. Ann.Med.Intern.Fenn. (1966); **55** (Suppl. 45): 7–55.

18. Sourander, L.B. and Kasanen, A. A 5-Year follow-up of bacteriuria in the aged. Gerontol.Clin. (1972); **14**: 274–281.

# Use of MULTISTIX* 10SG for the Diagnosis of Abdominal Pain in the Hospital Accident and Emergency Department

## Dr. R. McGlone

Accident and Emergency Department, Leeds General Infirmary
Present address: Consultant, Lancaster Royal Infirmary

It has been policy at the two main teaching hospitals in Leeds to send for urgent microscopy, all urine samples on patients presenting with abdominal pain. A previous study has suggested that the mid-stream specimen of urine (MSU) is of more value than a full blood count. However, to do urgent microscopy "out of normal hours" on all such patients has financial implications. Both sites together order 14 such tests a day, each one attracting a call-out fee for the technician. Also, the patient may have to wait longer in the Accident and Emergency Department until the mid-stream specimen of urine result is ready. In view of the latter, the Accident and Emergency nurse may order an MSU even before a doctor has seen the patient – "to save time".

*29% of MSU's in Accident & Emergency appeared totally irrelevant*

A survey of 669 mid-stream specimens of urine in the Accident and Emergency Department showed that 29% appeared totally irrelevant[1]!

*Microscopy can be used more selectively if strip testing is performed first*

To reduce the usage of urgent microscopy, urine testing strips could be usefully incorporated to screen out normal urines. However, this would be possible only if the number of false negatives were minimal. Several studies have shown this to be the case when done by laboratory staff[2,3,4,5]; indeed, the predictive value for negative growth was shown to be greater with strip testing (leucocyte esterase and/or nitrite): 94.9%, compared to 92% for microscopy[2]. This trend can be improved if photometry is used to read the strip test[4].

*The strip test missed less infected urines than did microscopy*

No similar study has been done in the Accident and Emergency Department, where there would be two important differences:

a. Urines would be freshly voided.
b. Nursing staff would be performing the test.

In view of the potential savings in time and cost, it was decided to assess the Ames MULTISTIX* 10SG reagent test strip at the Accident and Emergency Departments of the Leeds General Infirmary, and St James's University Hospital, Leeds.

### Reagent Strip Trials in the Accident and Emergency Department

The only previous study of the usefulness of the reagent strip in diagnosing urinary tract infections in the A & E environment was from the Royal Victoria Hospital, Montreal[6]. Fifty consecutive patients presenting to the department had their urines evaluated using both MULTISTIX 10SG and Combur-9 reagent strip tests by two physicians and the urines were sent for culture. There was no significant difference between the two tests in this small trial. The authors concluded that it was possible to rely upon the strip test to identify those patients with urinary tract infections, and hence restrict microscopic analysis.

Provisional results from a recent study based at the A & E departments of Leeds General Infirmary and St James's Hospital, confirmed that microscopy can be used more selectively.

A total of 1,112 patients presenting with abdominal pain were assessed using MULTISTIX 10SG strips. However, in our study, nursing staff – *NOT* physicians – visually read the strip. The strip was considered negative, if negative for blood, protein, nitrite and leucocyte esterase.

Appearance can be a good indicator of growth, but most samples were normal and very few turbid – only 4%. The frequency of other parameters is shown in *Table 1*.

## Table 1
### Frequency Distribution of Positive Reagent Strip Results in A & E

|  | % |
|---|---|
| Glucose | 4.0 |
| Ketone | 23.0 |
| Protein | 34.1 |
| (> "trace") | 17.6 |
| Blood | 40.8 |
| (> "trace") | 25.2 |
| Leucocytes | 28.3 |
| (> "trace") | 19.5 |
| Nitrite | 5.8 |
| Bilirubin | 7.3 |
| Urobilinogen | 2.5 |
| pH >7 | 14.7 |
| pH ≥8 | 8.8 |

There was a considerable incidence of positive results for many of the strip tests in this group of patients. Specific gravity peaked at 1.010 but skewed towards concentrated urine. The urine was orange/yellow in appearance in 16% of cases, which could account for a high (false) positive rate for bilirubin. Only in 8.6% of the infected urines was the pH >7.

When reagent strip and microscopy were assessed against laboratory culture, it showed that the reagent strip missed less infected urines and accurately predicted the absence of infection (*see Table 2*). Statistical terms are defined in the Appendix.

## Table 2
### Prediction of UTI Using Reagent Strips
– including all growth $\geq 10^5$

|  | Leucocyte Esterase % | Nitrite % | Blood % | Protein % | All 4 Parameters % | Microscopy >10 WBC % |
|---|---|---|---|---|---|---|
| Sensitivity | 66.1 | 39.2 | 66.9 | 57.9 | 89.5 | 70.5 |
| Specificity | 76.5 | 98.6 | 62.4 | 68.9 | 40.1 | 90.1 |
| Predictive Value for Negative Result | 94.5 | 92.6 | 93.5 | 92.6 | 96.4 | 96 |

If only significant growth is considered versus strip testing for all 4 parameters, then the sensitivity increases to 94.8% and the specificity is 39.9% (see *Table 3*).

| Table 3 Prediction of Clinically Significant Growth by Strip Testing | | |
|---|---|---|
| | Negative for Strip Testing | Microscopy >10 WBC |
| False Negatives for Significant Growth | 5 | 20 |
| Sensitivity | 94.8% | 81.1% |

Observer error and white cell lysis could account for the positive strips with negative microscopy. *If* we consider that >5 WBC per high field on microscopy indicates infection, there would have been 147 false positives and the A & E medical staff could have *wrongly ascribed the clinical findings to be due to a urinary tract infection*. *If* the significance level is >10 WBC per high field, then there would be 95 such patients – much less. However, pyuria in A & E patients may also be due to other causes, such as leucorrhoea in women.

The urines that were completely negative on strip testing totalled 396, i.e. 36.6% of the samples, which would have been a significant saving if these samples had not been sent for urgent microscopy. Only five of these patients had a significant urinary infection. If we examine these five patients more closely, we find that two complained of dysuria and the remaining three had less than 5 WBC per high field on microscopy. A significant infection was defined as positive culture with $\geq 10^5$ organisms/ml in either pure culture or mixed culture of not more than two species.

So far we have considered the detection of urinary tract infections. However, microscopy is also requested for the diagnosis of renal colic. The results of screening for haematuria are summarised in *Table 4*.

| Table 4 Reagent Strip Testing for Haematuria | |
|---|---|
| | % |
| Sensitivity | 79.5 |
| Specificity | 69.4 |
| Positive Predictive Value | 41.2 |
| Negative Predictive Value | 92.6 |

In practice, the commonest cause of haematuria was contamination of the urine due to menstruation. Strip testing failed to detect 47 patients who had microscopic haematuria, a disappointing result at first sight; however, all but seven had RBC $\leq 20$ cells/µl – below the sensitivity for the strip test.

The question to which we do not know the answer is – how many patients with renal colic were misdiagnosed because there was *no* haematuria on microscopy due to haemolysis?

## The Future

The addition of a photometer to read the reagent strip could improve the reliability of the test. This is now available.

Dip-inocculation culture has been successfully used in General Practice, and it would seem a possible alternative to "out of normal hours" urgent microscopy and plating. Indeed not all hospitals have urgent urine microscopy available, and in this present financial climate this situation may become the norm.

The task now is to convince hospital doctors that microscopy is not necessarily "a gold standard", and that strip testing is a valuable screening test to search for the "infected" urine. If this policy were accepted in A & E medicine, then there would be a reduction of 37% in requests for urgent microscopy.

*37% of urines need not be sent to the laboratory*

## References

1.  E.C. concerted Action Group, Leeds University. Mr de Dombal et al.

2.  S. Loo, et al. Urine screening strategy, employing dipstick analysis and selective culture: an evaluation. Am.J.Clin.Pathol. (1984); **81**: 634–642.

3.  Bank C, et al. Screening urine specimen populations for normality, using different dipsticks. J.Clin.Chem.Clin.Biochem. (1987); **25**: 299–307.

4.  Boreland P, et al. Dipstick analysis for screening of paediatric urine. J.Clin.Pathol. (1986); **39**: 1360–1362.

5.  Brown H. Chemical pre-screening of urines submitted for bacteriological, analysis. Med.Lab.Sci. (1988); **45**: 304–307.

6.  Shulman H. et al. p.199. Abstract; International Meeting of Accident and Emergency Meeting, 1988, Brisbane, Australia.

## Appendix:
## Statistical Terms

The sensitivity, specificity and predictive values for positive and negative strip tests were calculated as below.

$$\text{Sensitivity \%} = \frac{\text{true positive}}{\text{true positive} + \text{false negative}} \times 100$$

$$\text{Specificity \%} = \frac{\text{true negative}}{\text{true negative} + \text{false positive}} \times 100$$

$$\text{Predictive value for positive result \%} = \frac{\text{true positive}}{\text{true positive} + \text{false positive}} \times 100$$

$$\text{Predictive value for negative result \%} = \frac{\text{true negative}}{\text{true negative} + \text{false negative}} \times 100$$

# Bladder Cancer and Haematuria

**Mr. J.P. Britton**

Tutor in Urology, St. James's University Hospital, Leeds
Present address: Department of Urology, Guy's Hospital, London

### Incidence

There are almost 7,000 new cases of bladder cancer each year in the UK

Bladder cancer now ranks as the sixth commonest malignant disease in the United Kingdom, with almost 7,000 new cases each year. During the past 30 years, the incidence and the annual number of reported deaths due to the disease have risen considerably. A general practice with a list size of 5,000 patients will see about one new case each year, but will also have 5 patients currently under treatment for the disease. Bladder cancer most commonly presents in elderly men and is rare under the age of 40 years.

---

**Table 1**
**Bladder Cancer**

- Sixth commonest malignant disease in the UK
- 1.5 new cases per annum per 1,000 men over the age of 60 years
- Male : female ratio 2.5 : 1
- Increased risk with smoking and industrial carcinogens

---

### Aetiology

The association between smoking and bladder cancer is well documented, with up to a fourfold increased risk for male smokers. Occupational exposure to certain chemicals, typically those encountered in the dye and organic chemical manufacturing industries, is also of importance and may account for up to one quarter of the total number of bladder cancers in the male population.

### Presentation

Patients with painless gross haematuria must be considered to have a bladder tumour until proven otherwise

Although most tumours bleed in an occult manner, the majority of patients present with painless gross haematuria. The visible bleeding rarely persists for more than a few hours or days and may not occur again for several weeks, but all such patients must be considered to have a bladder tumour until proved otherwise.

More difficult are the patients presenting with urinary frequency and urgency – less specific indicators of neoplasia, but more common in cases of carcinoma *in situ*. In such cases, the presence of microscopic haematuria or atypical cytology may alert the clinician to the possibility of a bladder tumour and indicate a need for urgent cystoscopy.

---

**Table 2**
**Presentation of Bladder Cancer**

- Painless haematuria
- Microscopic haematuria
- Less commonly:
  - urgency
  - frequency
  - dysuria

---

### Pathology, Staging and Prognosis

Most bladder tumours are transitional cell carcinomas. They are classified according to the histological grade and depth of invasion. The well differentiated lesions are usually papillary and superficial, whilst the poorly differentiated tumours are usually solid and invasive. The superficial tumours, although often multiple and recurring locally in the bladder, follow a relatively benign course and only 15 per cent progress to become invasive[1]. Solid tumours have a much worse prognosis, and often have metastasised by the time of presentation[2].

### Treatment

Most superficial tumours are easily treated by a combination of transurethral resection and cystodiathermy, but patients require regular review cystoscopies over many years to maintain control of the disease. HEMASTIX* reagent strip tests can be used in combination with urine cytology for monitoring recurrence, although they may fail to detect some small, well differentiated tumours which do not bleed.

Invasive tumours are treated by cystectomy and/or radiotherapy, but the 5-year survival for those deemed treatable is no more than 40 per cent.

| Table 3 Bladder Tumours | |
| --- | --- |
| **Well differentiated tumours** | – usually superficial |
| | – rarely invade |
| | – local treatment |
| | – good prognosis |
| **Poorly differentiated tumours** | – usually invasive |
| | – metastases common |
| | – cystectomy ± radiotherapy |
| | – poor prognosis |

### Screening for Bladder Cancer

Despite advances within the fields of surgery, radiotherapy and chemotherapy, the survival figures for bladder cancer have shown little change over 30 years. At the moment, our only hope of improving the prognosis may lie with early detection by screening, to give the present treatment options a better opportunity of eradicating the disease. Screening aims to identify disease at an early stage by a method that is simple, cheap, reliable and acceptable to the population. Methods that have been used for screening in bladder cancer include:

1. urine cytology
2. detection of microhaematuria

### 1. Urine Cytology

Urine cytology has been used for many years as a method of detecting urothelial cancer in high-risk groups, particularly in workers exposed to industrial carcinogens. It has been shown that tumours diagnosed by malignant cell cytology tend more frequently to be stage 1 than tumours which present with signs or symptoms, and this results in a better overall survival[3]. However, although good at detecting poorly differentiated tumours and carcinoma *in situ*, the diagnostic accuracy is very much reduced when looking for more well-differentiated lesions. Urine cytology has not been shown to be a useful screening procedure in the general population.

## 2. Microhaematuria

Detection of the occult bleeding or microhaematuria associated with the presence of a bladder tumour offers the simplest method of screening for bladder cancer. The small amounts of blood can be easily detected by urinary reagent strips, and investigation of the patients with microhaematuria will reveal a bladder tumour in 1–10%[4-8]. However, some lesions may be missed because not all tumours shed red cells into the urine all the time. My own recent studies, and those of others[9], have shown that occult bleeding, like gross haematuria, is often intermittent, both in patients with bladder tumours and in patients without known disease. Thus, it may be suggested that the sensitivity of this method of screening could be improved by performing repeated urine tests over a period of time rather than relying on a single test. This hypothesis is currently being investigated. Other tumour markers which could possibly be used for screening have been identified in the urine of patients with bladder cancer, including carcinoembryonic antigen, fibrinogen degradation products and other tumour-specific antigens and proteins. Their clinical usefulness in the detection and evaluation of bladder cancer has yet to be fully established, but a diagnostic accuracy greater than that of urine cytology has not been demonstrated.

### Investigation of Microhaematuria

A suggested algorithm for investigation of reagent strip haematuria in men is shown in *Figure 1*. Urine microscopy isolates the small number of patients with red cell casts pathognomonic of glomerular bleeding requiring investigation for renal disease. Urine cytology identifies those patients with atypical cells needing full investigation by intravenous urography and rigid cystoscopy under general anaesthesia. However, both intravenous urography and rigid cystoscopy have a small, but definite, morbidity and are perhaps not justified in the patient with normal urine cytology in whom the chance of finding a urothelial tumour is only relatively small. Renal ultrasound offers a satisfactory alternative as a means of diagnosing a renal mass; the introduction of the flexible cystoscope allows outpatient endoscopy under local anaesthesia. Transitional cell carcinomas of the upper tracts are uncommon, but if present, may be missed.

### The Future

It is hoped that public education about the hazards of smoking and legislation concerning the use of industrial carcinogens will help to halt the rise in incidence of bladder cancer. Until improved methods of treatment are identified, early detection of the disease offers the only hope of improving its prognosis. Endeavours to isolate a more specific tumour marker to identify disease and predict progression continue.

### Conclusions

Urinary reagent strip tests offer a quick, simple and inexpensive method of identifying a group of patients with an "increased chance" of having a bladder

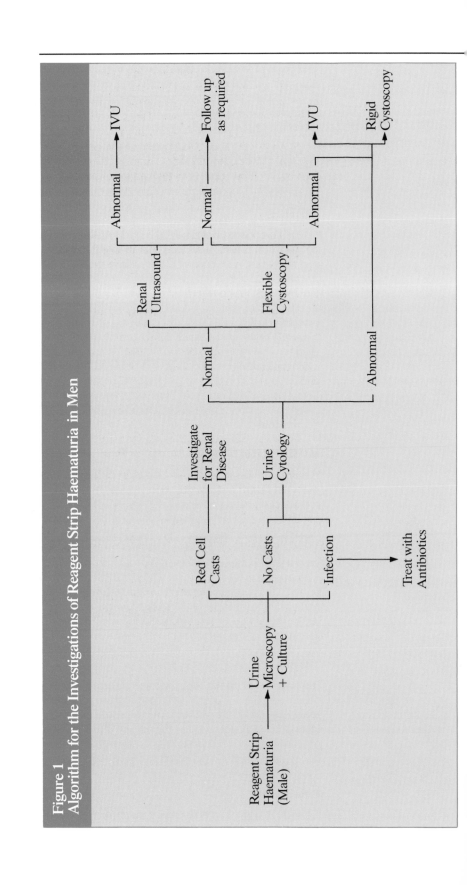

**Figure 1**
Algorithm for the Investigations of Reagent Strip Haematuria in Men

tumour. Using HEMASTIX, the test can be easily performed in the health centre or the outpatient clinic and, in our experience, HEMASTIX can be easily used by the patient at home after adequate instruction. It is suggested that the sensitivity of urinary reagent strips for detecting bladder cancer may be improved by performing repeated tests rather than by relying on a single test. The use of reagent strips, in association with urine cytology and flexible cystoscopy, offers a feasible method of screening for bladder cancer. They offer the patient and doctor the opportunity of diagnosing bladder cancer at an earlier stage, with the subsequent better chance of survival.

## References

1. Gilbert, H.A., Logan, J.L., Kagan, A.R. et al. The natural history of papillary transitional cell carcinoma of the bladder and its treatment in an unselected population on the basis of histologic grading. J.Urol. (1978); **119**: 488–492.

2. Hopkins, S.C., Ford, K.S. and Soloway, M.S. Invasive bladder cancer: support for screening. J.Urol. (1983); **130**: 61–63.

3. Cartwright, R.A., Gadian, T., Garland, J.B. and Bernard, S.M. The influence of malignant cell cytology screening on the survival of industrial bladder cancer cases. J.Epidemiol.Comm.Health (1981): 35–38.

4. Greene, L.F., O'Shaughnessy E.J. and Hendricks, E.D. Study of five hundred patients with asymptomatic microhaematuria. J.A.M.A. (1956); **161**: 610–614.

5. Carson, C.C., Segura, J.W. and Greene, L.F. Clinical importance of microhaematuria. J.A.M.A. (1979); **241**: 149–150.

6. Golin, A.L. and Howard, R.S. Asymptomatic microscopic haematuria. J.Urol. (1980); **124**: 389–391.

7. Ritchie, C.D., Bevan, E.A. and Collier, St J. Importance of occult haematuria found at screening. Brit.Med.J. (1986); **292**: 681–683.

8. Thompson, I.M. The evaluation of microscopic haematuria: a population based study. J.Urol. (1987); **138**: 1189–1190.

9. Messing, E.M., Young, T.B., Hunt, V.B., Emoto, S.E. and Wehbie, J.M. The significance of asymptomatic microhaematuria in men 50 or more years old: findings of a home screening study using urinary dipsticks. J.Urol. (1987); **137**: 919–922.

# Peri-Operative Urine Testing

**Dr. I.T. Campbell**

**Senior Lecturer in Anaesthesia,** University of Liverpool

Present address: University Department of Anaesthesia, Withington Hospital, Manchester.

### Pre-Operative Urine Testing

Over 3 million operations are carried out in the National Health Service each year. Many patients undergoing surgery have intercurrent disease which, although not directly related to the operation, may result in complications. Such conditions include, obviously enough, respiratory and cardiac problems, but also renal and hepatic conditions as well as diabetes. Complications resulting from intercurrent illness may prolong recovery from surgery, and result in an extended stay in hospital involving other specialties, use of laboratory facilities, further investigations, etc. Normally, if the condition is known, problems can be anticipated and complications avoided.

Many patients undergoing surgery have intercurrent disease, which may result in complications

## Table 1
## Indications for Pre-Operative Urine Testing

| Urine Test | Indications |
|---|---|
| Bilirubin  Urobilinogen | Jaundice and Hepatitis |
| Glucose | Diabetes mellitus |
| Ketones | Ketoacidosis |
| Protein | Renal disease |
| Blood | Renal or lower urinary tract disease |
| Leucocytes | Renal disease |

Intercurrent medical disease thus affects anaesthetic and surgical management. It may even affect the decision of whether or not, or at least when, to operate, but more often it influences the techniques used. The condition may be well defined and in the process of being treated, or it may only be revealed on the routine history and examination undertaken by the house staff. Alternatively, it may not be clinically obvious at all. The house surgeon usually orders supplementary investigations if these are deemed appropriate – ECG, chest X-ray, blood tests, etc. For many patients this may be the first full medical examination they have had for years, and there is a temptation to use it to screen them for all sorts of conditions, doing a chest X-ray, ECG and a full biochemical blood screen on everybody regardless of age, or symptomatology. This is particularly so in these days of computer controlled, multichannel analysers, when sending 10ml of blood to the laboratory may produce serum concentrations of 20 or more substances.

There is a need to identify disease that may influence anaesthetic and surgical management, or which may adversely affect the patient's health

Whatever the need to screen the general population for occult disease, there must be a more appropriate time to do it than on admission to hospital for elective surgery. There is certainly a need to identify disease that may influence anaesthetic and surgical management, or which may adversely affect the patient's health if it is not recognised, but routinely doing laboratory tests on everyone can raise more problems than it solves – particularly in relation to multiple biochemical investigations. Laboratory reference ranges are usually determined by that range within which 95% of a normal population falls[1]. This means that if a biochemical screen is done for 20 substances – Na, K, phosphate, creatinine, etc – on average one result in every normal patient will fall outside of that range. Faced with an abnormal result the night before an operation, a clinician is faced with 2 choices – one is to repeat the test and perhaps postpone the operation; the other is to ignore the result. In most instances an unexpected result will ultimately turn out to be of no significance or even spurious. To postpone surgery on the eve of an operation has major financial implications for the hospital, as well as causing inconvenience and unnecessary anxiety to the patient. If the result of a test is ignored, one might reasonably question the wisdom of doing it in the first place.

The commoner diseases affecting anaesthetic and surgical management which may not be clinically obvious but which could be identified biochemically, are renal and hepatic impairment and diabetes mellitus. Renal and hepatic disease should be identified pre-operatively, because many drugs are metabolised and excreted by these routes, and because unknowingly subjecting somebody with renal or hepatic disease to major surgery can result in further deterioration in organ function or even overt failure[2,3,4].

*Renal and hepatic disease should be identified pre-operatively*

The incidence of elevated aminotransferases in the general population is in the region of between 1 and 10%[1,5,6,7,8]. Most are due to a high alcohol intake or medication, or are of uncertain clinical significance. The liver has a large functional reserve, and patients with mild liver disease usually tolerate anaesthesia and surgery well[4]. Severe liver disease should be evident clinically. The greatest danger is of operating unknowingly on someone incubating viral hepatitis[9,10], particularly with the ongoing controversy about so-called "halothane hepatitis"[11].

*There is great danger in operating unknowingly on someone incubating viral hepatitis*

Renal disease is notoriously asymptomatic[2]. In the general population the incidence of impaired renal function, as denoted by an elevated serum creatinine or urea, is less than 1% under the age of 40, rising to 3–5% over 60[6,8,12,13].

The greatest danger in diabetes is hypoglycaemia occurring under, and being masked by, general anaesthesia, although this is more likely to occur in the diabetic being treated with insulin than it is in the unrecognised diabetic. In the unrecognised diabetic, the problem is that of subjecting a patient on the verge of ketoacidosis to a prolonged surgical procedure.

*The greatest danger in diabetes is hypoglycaemia occurring under general anaesthetic*

All of these conditions can be recognised on blood testing. However, routine biochemical screening of everyone scheduled for surgery is expensive and, as outlined above, produces its own problems. Routine urine testing is simpler, cheaper and should be adequate to ensure that the patients at risk are identified[14]. It would also identify patients in the early stages of viral hepatitis. Bilirubin and, transiently, urobilinogen often appear in the urine before the onset of jaundice, so urine testing offers a satisfactory alternative to a blood test[15].

*Routine urine screening is simpler and less expensive than blood tests*

*Bilirubin and urobilinogen may precede jaundice*

As with all investigations, urine testing may produce some positive results which ultimately turn out to be spurious or of no clinical significance. When an unexpected result is obtained with a urine test, however, it is easily repeatable.

In contrast, to repeat a blood test usually involves the laboratory as well as a further venepuncture.

The incidence of an elevated serum creatinine in patients over the age of 50 is such that, in this age group, it is almost certainly worthwhile measuring serum creatinine routinely. Below this age it is probably not cost-effective, but the existence of pre-existing renal disease should be identified on urine examination by the presence of protein, blood or pyuria on strip testing; this can be followed up by a serum creatinine test if necessary. For the otherwise fit and healthy individual under 50, the routine urine test should be the only biochemical test necessary. Steps must be taken, however, to ensure that the test is carried out correctly[16,17], and that the surgical and anaesthetic staff are aware of the results[18].

*Surgical and anaesthetic staff must be aware of the urine test results*

### Post-Operative Urine Testing

*The specific gravity strip test may indicate the state of hydration post-operatively*

Post-operative routine urine testing by strip tests may also reveal useful information. The recent development of strips to monitor specific gravity may give some indication of the state of hydration, particularly after major procedures in which large fluid shifts occur. The presence or absence of glucose in the urine can be used to monitor patients having intravenous nutritional support, and would also identify patients with mild diabetes and only a small degree of glucose intolerance pre-operatively but which may be exacerbated by the stress of surgery. Monitoring urinary ketones serves the same purpose. The presence of small quantities of ketones in the urine, however, may be perfectly normal – particularly if the patient has been starved for longer than 24 or 48 hours. It merely denotes that endogenous stores of carbohydrate have become exhausted, and that the patient has switched over to metabolising fat. Some have regarded the early appearance of mild ketonuria as representing an entirely appropriate and even a beneficial adaptation to the joint insults of surgical or traumatic injury and starvation[19]. Such a viewpoint however, is still controversial.

## Table 2
### Indications for Urine Testing Post-Operatively

| Urine Test | Indications |
| --- | --- |
| Specific Gravity | State of hydration |
| Glucose | Monitor IV nutritional support |
|  | Identify mild diabetics, exacerbated by the stress |
| Ketones | Identify mild diabetics, exacerbated by surgery |
|  | Endogenous carbohydrate stores exhausted |
|  | Normal response to surgery |

## References

1. Friedman G.D., Goldberg M., Ahja J.N., Siegelaub A.B., Bassis M.L., Collen M.I. Biochemical screening tests. Effects of panel size on medical care. Arch.Int.Med. (1972); **129**: 91–97.

2. Bevan D.R. Renal function in anaesthesia and surgery. London: Academic Press, (1979).

3. Strunin L. The Liver and anaesthesia, London; W.B. Saunders Company Ltd., (1977).

4. Bastron, R.D. Hepatic and Renal Physiology. In: Miller, R.D. Anaesthesia. Churchill Livingstone, New York, (1981); pp 763–94.

5. Ahlvin R.C. Biochemical screening – a critique. New Eng.J.Med. (1970); **283**: 1084–6.

6. Collen M.F., Feldman R., Siegelaub A.B., Crawford D. Dollar cost per positive test for automated multiphasic screening. New Eng.J.Med. (1970); **283**: 459–63.

7. Ezeoke A.C. Biochemical studies of apparently "healthy" blood donors with reference to liver function tests and immunoglobulins. Ric.Clin.Lab.(1985); **15**: 267–73.

8. Schneiderman L.J., De Salvo L., Baylor S., Wolf P.L. The "abnormal" screening laboratory result. Its effect on physician and patient. Arch.Int.Med. (1972); **129**: 88–90.

9. Wataneeyawech M., Kelly K.A. Hepatic diseases unsuspected before surgery. NY State J.Med. (1975); **75**: 1278–81.

10. Schemel W.H. Unexpected hepatic dysfunction found by multiple laboratory screening. Anesth.Analg. – Curr.Res. (1976); **55**: 810–12.

11. Blogg C.E. Editorial: Halothane and the liver: the problem revisited and made obsolete. Br.Med.J. (1986); **292**: 1691–2.

12. Jacobsen J., Bach A.B., Dalsgaard P.F. Blood tests before elective surgery. Anaesthesia (1987); **42**: 78–79.

13. Carmalt M.H.B., Freeman P., Stephens A.J.H., Whitehead T.P. Value of routine multiple blood tests in patients attending the general practitioner. Br.Med.J. (1970); **i**: 620–3.

14. Campbell I.T., Gosling P. Editorial: Preoperative biochemical screening. Br.Med.J.(1988); **297**: 803–4.

15. Jones E.A., Berk P.D. Liver function. In: Brown S.S., Mitchell F.L., Young D.S., eds. Chemical Diagnosis of Disease. Amsterdam: Elsevier and North Holland Biomedical Press, (1979); 525–662.

16. Fraser C.G. Urine analysis: current performance and strategies for improvement. Br.Med.J. (1985); **291**: 321–25.

17. Kirkland, J.A., Morgan H.G. An assessment of routine hospital testing for protein and glucose. Scot.Med.J. (1961); **6**: 513–19.

18. Hoffbrand B.I. Preoperative biochemical screening. Br.Med.J. (1988); **297**: 1270.

19. Editorial: Beneficial ketosis. Lancet. (1973); **2**: 366.

# Urine Strip Testing in Toxicology

## Dr. D. J. Berry

Principal Biochemist, National Poisons Unit, New Cross Hospital, London

The testing of blood and urine samples for the presence of drugs has become an important activity both for specialist toxicology and general biochemistry laboratories. Apart from the quantitative analyses which are done to monitor therapy, there are two main reasons for examining biological specimens to see whether drugs are present (*Table 1*):

1. To investigate a comatosed, drowsy, or confused patient, in order to see whether the symptoms may be drug-induced.

2. To screen asymptomatic patients in order to see whether they are ingesting drugs.

The latter requirement arises for several different reasons:

–   To assess drug dependent patients, both for purposes of preliminary evaluation, and also treatment monitoring by checking that prescribed drugs are being complied with and illicit substance use has discontinued.

–   To test that patients who are particularly susceptible to poor compliance (psychiatric, elderly, etc.) are taking the medication prescribed to them.

–   Testing for drug use in employees and candidates for employment.

–   Testing for drug abuse in sport.

Therefore, it can be seen that a considerable amount of drug testing is undertaken for a variety of reasons.

---

**Table 1**
**Indications for Testing Urine for the Presence of Drugs**

| | |
|---|---|
| **In a comatose, drowsy or confused patient.** | Are these symptoms induced by drugs? |
| **Screening asymptomatic patients.** | Are they ingesting drugs? |
| **Monitoring drug therapy.** | |

---

### Symptomatic (Especially Comatose) Patients

Patients may become unconscious as a result of a variety of clinical conditions, and drug-related coma is not an uncommon problem in the United Kingdom. In such cases, there is often strong circumstantial evidence of drug ingestion, but even when this is present one should not rule out the possibility of another cause for the patient's condition. As soon as a urine sample becomes available, it should be tested at the bedside by MULTISTIX* 8SG, particularly with respect to pH, protein, glucose and ketones (*Table 2*).

At the same time, a blood sample should be despatched to the laboratory for biochemical testing. These tests allow the rapid detection of glycosuria and

*A urine sample should be tested at the bedside with MULTISTIX 8SG as soon as the sample becomes available*

ketonuria in a comatosed diabetic. However, a positive result for ketones may indicate intoxication by acetone or isopropyl alcohol, as an alternative to starvation or diabetic ketosis.

| **Table 2** | |
|---|---|
| **Routine Urine Reagent Strip Testing in Toxicology** | |
| **Test** | **Indication** |
| pH | Presence of some drugs and poisons which produce an acid urine<br>To determine whether a sample is "genuine" |
| Protein | Renal impairment<br>Side-effect of certain drugs |
| Glucose | Diabetes in a comatose patient<br>Side-effect of certain drugs |
| Ketones | Ketoacidotic comatose diabetic<br>Starvation<br>Intoxication by acetone or isopropyl alcohol |

One must be aware that some drugs may cause slight abnormalities in biochemical testing, e.g. thiazide diuretics can produce glycosuria, and some patients being treated with anti-rheumatoid drugs may develop proteinuria.

An acid pH may indicate the presence of certain drugs or poisons

Some drugs, such as salicylates, and poisons, such as methanol and ethylene glycol, may affect the pH, producing an acid urine. The urine pH may also be an indication of whether a specimen from an apparently healthy person is indeed a "true" sample, or has been tampered with in an attempt to disguise irregularities.

PHENISTIX may presumptively identify certain drugs

In addition, PHENISTIX* reagent strips can be used to screen for the presence of certain drugs in urine, such as salicylates, some phenothiazines, and some antibiotics, since documented and defined typical and atypical colours result when they are present. These are listed in *Table 3*. Negative PHENISTIX tests demonstrate that these drugs are absent. However, if a definite colour reaction occurs, then confirmatory testing should be undertaken in the laboratory.

| Table 3 Interpretation of PHENISTIX Colours | |
|---|---|
| **Colour Produced** | **Drug** |
| **Grey-Green and Green** | Phenylpyruvic Acid |
| **Brown and Red** | Para-Aminosalicylic Acid, Aspirin and other Salicylates |
| **Brown, Red or Purple** | Sulphonamides (some) Tetracyclines (some) |
| **Brown** | Homogentisic Acid |
| **Pink, Red or Purple** | Phenothiazines (some) |

**Illicit Drug Use**

Prior to testing urines for illicit drugs, it is vital to establish that the sample has not been tampered with in any way. Patients will sometimes attempt to dilute their urine sample, either directly with tap water, or by ingesting diuretics in order to decrease the concentration of drug in the sample below the detection limit of the testing method. Therefore, any urine sample which is to be examined for illicit drugs should first be tested in the toxicology laboratory by MULTISTIX 8SG for specific gravity, to establish that it is a bona fide specimen.

*Any urine to be examined for illicit drugs should first be tested by MULTISTIX 8SG for specific gravity*

Having tested the samples for biochemical abnormalities, either in a side room or the laboratory, and having obtained negative results, the urine can then be examined for the presence of drugs. This is performed by a range of immunological and chromatographic assay methods, which can screen to detect a wide range of drugs that are commonly taken in overdose or used illicitly. These tests must be able not only to detect the high concentrations of drugs which are often present in a coma case, but also the lower levels which one finds in normal therapeutic use. If a drug is detected in the urine of an unconscious patient, one would normally proceed to determine the concentration in plasma, in order to gauge the severity of overdose or to guide therapy, although active treatment is only rarely applied in these cases.

**Conclusions**

*Reagent strip testing is important in eliminating other common causes of coma in an acute setting*

In summary, the testing of patients for drug ingestion has become an important part of managing a variety of clinical problems. In an acute setting, it is necessary initially to preclude other more common causes of coma and strip testing has an important role to play in this, allowing the clinician to take immediate action where this is indicated. When urine samples are being examined for evidence of drug misuse, it is vital to establish the validity of the sample. In this way, the clinician can be confident that the testing system will be able to detect the low concentrations of drugs and metabolites which may be present in these cases, and can respond accordingly.

# Urine Screening in General Practice

**Dr. P. R. Elliott**
General Practitioner, Buntingford, Hertfordshire

### Screening

The concept of General Practitioners' screening and practising preventative medicine is gaining ground.

We are looking for an acceptable simple test that detects "disease" at an early stage in its known clinical course, when treatment is beneficial.

The Government's latest "Analysis" of the Health Service in its White Paper sees GP preventative medicine as a viable way forward. Screening is already practised in many spheres, and urine screening is a routine part of ante-natal care and hospital visits. Should this be extended more widely? Defined criteria for screening are important, and urine screening fulfills those criteria listed in *Table 1*, as suggested by Wilson[1] 25 years ago.

*Urine screening fulfils defined criteria*

---

**Table 1**
**Criteria for Screening**

1. The disease must constitute an important problem.
2. The disease must have an accepted treatment.
3. The facilities for diagnosis and treatment must be available.
4. There must be a recognisable latent or early symptom stage.
5. Suitable tests or examinations must be possible. They must be quick and simple to perform, reproducible, sufficiently accurate, relatively inexpensive.
6. The test must be acceptable to the population.
7. The natural history of the disease must be understood.
8. There must be an agreed policy on treatment.
9. The cost must be related to other medical care expenditure.
10. Screening must be a continuous process.

---

In our Practice we have a Nurse Practitioner, active in a screening role and we have set up a screening programme based on the Oxford M.O.T. System[2], for patients aged 20–65, using a risk score.

All patients between the ages of 20 and 65 who attend the surgery are offered a letter explaining the screening system. They can read this while they wait to see the GP, who can then reinforce the message. On leaving the surgery they are offered an appointment with the Nurse Practitioner. The letter also requests them to bring an early-morning urine sample to the screening.

Patients who have been screened have a blue sticker placed on their notes with the dates of screening. When notes are being prepared for surgery, the appointment book is 'highlighted' for patients who do not have a sticker, and these patients are offered screening letters when they attend.

Patients attending for screening have their blood pressure, peak flow, diet and history checked, and their urine sample is tested using N-LABSTIX* reagent strips and, more recently, MULTISTIX* 10SG tests, including protein, glucose, ketones, pH, blood and nitrite. If there are any abnormalities, the sample is sent to the laboratory for confirmation and the Nurse Practitioner may consult the doctor for immediate treatment, if this seems necessary.

When the laboratory report is returned, the Nurse Practitioner checks on any abnormalities and arranges for further samples to be tested, or other follow-up as appropriate.

Patients over 65 are screened at home, also by the Nurse Practitioner. The over 65's have problems they do not consider "worth bothering the doctor with". When these are detected and treated, there is often a considerable improvement in "quality of life".

A list of over 65's has been grouped by age, and also by how well they are known to the practice team. The Nurse Practitioner aims to visit 3 patients a week, and the letter confirming her visit asks the patient to keep a urine sample for her. These are, again, tested using N-LABSTIX.

To date, 24% of elderly patients screened have had abnormalities on urinalysis. Several of these have been "non-reproducible" protein particularly, but a number were unrecognised urinary tract infections. It was only after the test result was mentioned that several of these patients admitted to incontinence symptoms. These were relieved by appropriate antibiotics.

The microscope may, of course, still be useful to GP's who can remember how to use one. For most of us, however, N-LABSTIX or MULTISTIX 10SG is all we need.

Any abnormalities, from either set of screening, are followed up by the Nurse Practitioner using pre-arranged and agreed protocols. Details are held on computer and follow-up letters are sent, as necessary.

Urine screening also takes place in the ante-natal clinic at each visit. URISTIX* (glucose/protein) are traditionally used, but at least once in early pregnancy N-LABSTIX or MULTISTIX 10SG is used to screen for infection.

### Results

Results from the current screening programmes are presented in *Table 2*. In addition to this study, 279 males and 375 females aged 5 years or above, had been previously screened, which produced the clinical findings listed in *Table 3*. Urine testing has revealed a variety of disorders, including urinary tract infections, diabetes, and a bladder papilloma.

| Table 2<br>**Results from Current Screening** | | |
|---|---|---|
| Age: 20–65    Male    351<br>Female    287 | | |
| 10 nitrite positive | – | UTI treated. |
| 5 protein positive | – | 3 negative on retest |
| 14 blood positive | – | 1 referred to hospital,<br>10 with infection,<br>3 negative on retest. |
| 3 glucose positive | – | one diabetic, two GTT<br>renal glycosuria. |

| Table 3 | |
|---|---|
| **Results from Previous Urine Screening** | |
| Unknown diabetes | 3 |
| Borderline glycosuria | 1 |
| Poor control of diabetes | 3 |
| Papilloma of bladder | 1 |
| Unknown urinary tract infection | 19 |
| Confirmed urinary tract infection | 5 |
| Persistent proteinuria – under investigation | 10 |
| Persistent haematuria – under investigation | 6 |

### Value of Urine Screening

Urine screening is relevant to the patient, in early detection of disease which can cause complications – such as diabetes, or be fatal – such as malignancy. Most patients appreciate the chance of early detection, but some still bury their heads in the sand!

Early detection of abnormalities will lead to earlier treatment and, in many cases, this can be of great benefit. One of our cases, a 20-year-old female with diabetes, was detected before any complications had arisen and so, hopefully, early treatment will prevent long-term complications of the disease.

As a GP, there is a great sense of satisfaction in being "on top" of the caseload and knowing that all is well – or that disease is being detected early. The team approach is also a great strength, and benefits doctor and patient alike.

Is screening cost effective? The use of N-LABSTIX will, hopefully, prevent "negative" or non-infected urine samples being sent to the laboratory. If a urine sample – particularly an early morning specimen – is clear on testing with N-LABSTIX or similar test strips, it is unlikely that the laboratory will detect any abnormality. Early detection will mean simpler treatment which will, hopefully, be less expensive.

New Government initiatives to be introduced in General Practice mean that GP's will have to become even more conscious of the cost of laboratory tests. There is also likely to be increasing control over the availability of such tests to the GP, so that using these reagent strips will allow a greater degree of freedom to practice good medicine.

### Whither Urine Screening?

There are several interesting future developments in urine screening and, as a practice, we are beginning to try MULTISTIX 8SG and MULTISTIX 10SG reagent strips.

The additional provision of a "leucocyte" count seems to be catching those patients with a UTI who are nitrite negative. Sometimes a positive leucocyte test can indicate inflammation rather than infection. If the urine is sent for culture, or a dipslide is used, this will enable the two conditions to be differentiated.

The "Bile" test is also very interesting, although not often positive at present in our experience. Bile pigment testing, for example, can be used as part of a simple bedside investigation of patients with jaundice[3], which may be enough to

*Urine screening is relevant to the patient in the early detection of disease*

*A 20-year-old newly diagnosed diabetic may now avoid long-term complications*

*Early detection will mean simpler treatment and should be cost-effective*

*Using reagent strips allows the GP a greater degree of freedom to practice good medicine*

*Bile pigment testing in jaundiced patients may clinch the diagnosis or determine a course of action*

clinch the diagnosis, or at least determine if a surgical or medical referral is needed.

The specific gravity test is nothing short of amazing! Those of us who remember struggling with hydrometers or measuring cylinders, and diluting urine if the sample was insufficient, then what *WAS* the factor to multiply by again . . . ?

Now to have the SG read out on a small block on a strip is unbelievable! As the SG test is more accessible it will, no doubt, be used more often as a measure of renal function, i.e. the ability to concentrate urine. Allowance must be made for fluid intake etc, but a "random" or "fasting" reading of 1.020 or more is acceptable as normal. All that remains, really, is the development of the "smart" stick, that can be plugged into a computer terminal giving a readout of the likely diagnosis and the most useful treatment regime.

Throw away those microscopes – invest in some MULTISTIX 10SG strips!

### References

1.  Wilson, J.M.G., Some principles of early diagnosis and treatment in surveillance and early diagnosis in general practice. Teeling-Smith, G., Office of Health Economics (1965).

2.  Fullard, E., Fowler, G., Gray, M. Facilitating prevention in primary care. Br.Med.J. (1984); **289**: 1585.

3.  Longmore, J.M., Bedside tests in a patient with jaundice. Update (1989), p.418.

# Quality Assurance in Urine Testing: The Role of the Hospital Pharmacy

## Dr. M. C. Allwood
Principal Pharmacist, Addenbrookes Hospital, Cambridge
Present Address: Royal Infirmary, Derby

### Purchase and Supply

In the early days of urine testing at the bedside, clinical staff were required to mix urine samples with appropriate reagent solutions. These reagents were normally supplied by the pharmacy departments, where they were manufactured. When reagent tablets became available commercially, for urine sugar testing, the pharmacy continued to be the purchaser and distributor for all ward-based urine-testing reagents. Thus, while not categorisable as drugs or medicines, reagent materials in a ready-to-use form continued to be integrated into the pharmaceutical service.

For a number of reasons it is essential that the provision of urine test reagents, be they solutions, tablets or strips, is controlled and co-ordinated within a hospital. For example, the availability on a ward of more than one type or brand of urine test strip can be hazardous. Each brand will require different use protocols, colour interpretation, and possibly instrumentation. Confusion will be an inevitable consequence if more than one type is available to nursing or medical staff. Adequate staff training and familiarity with the recommended reagent brand is crucial to accurate interpretation of tests.

### Choice of Supply

*A product must achieve an acceptable level of performance on the ward or clinic*

While cost and company support are of importance in governing choice of a supplier of reagent tablet or strip, it is clearly essential to ensure that any product will achieve an acceptable level of performance on the ward or clinic. The technical aspects of any strip need to be fully assessed before purchase is considered. A number of aspects must be examined.

Acceptable levels of precision, accuracy and reproducibility are obviously the primary consideration. It is essential that the biochemistry service satisfies itself that any brand of product can achieve acceptable performance criteria both in the laboratory and in the hands of the user. The product must be assessed by the users for ease of use, interpretation and acceptability. It is important to ensure that the particular item can be applied to the diagnostic task by those responsible for its use in practice.

Packaging of each item must be considered by the pharmacy and biochemistry departments. This should take into account both the physical and chemical protection provided, especially during storage on the ward or clinic, and the nature and size of the outer packs, which will govern demands for storage space, and wastage.

### Pharmacies' Hospital Role

Decisions regarding choice and purchase of urine reagent tests are normally made every two years by Health Authorities. But changes are rare because of difficulty in moving stock and retraining. After purchase, there are a number of important roles for a modern hospital pharmacy in helping to ensure safe, effective and economical use of reagent strips and tablets.

### Supply to Wards and Clinics

Reagent tablets and strips are included as a standard stock item for all wards and clinics using them. They may be supplied from the pharmacy through a

Stock must be rotated so that older items are used before more recent stock ward medicines distribution system or a technician-operated top-up service, to ensure that adequate stocks are maintained. It is essential that stock levels are kept as low as possible, and that stock is rotated so that older items are used before more recent stock is commenced. Regular visits by the technician or the ward pharmacist should ensure that good stock-keeping habits are maintained.

The manufacturer may ᴐvide a useful ward service and technical support The manufacturer or supplier may also provide a useful ward service, especially in staff training and technical support. Pharmacy staff can also ensure that any out-of-date material is removed immediately from use. Short-dated items can be recirculated via the pharmacy.

**Storage on the Ward**

It is essential that reagent strips and tablets are packaged to provide physical protection, avoid light or moisture penetration during storage, and provide a readily resealable cap to ensure that the contents are protected from exposure to moisture throughout its shelf life.

Staff do not always replace the bottle cap tightly – or at all – leading to deterioration It is common practice to store and use urine reagent strips in the sluice room, a relatively humid environment. It is essential that the bottle closure prevents moisture penetration and is readily resealed after each opening. Tests on strips stored on wards have shown that staff do not always reclose caps tightly after each use. Evidence of significant deterioration of urine test strips has been discovered, and is due to poor re-closure after each use, or even forgetting to replace the cap after opening. Moisture therefore enters the container, rapidly saturates the desiccant and then causes strip deterioration. It is also important to ensure good stock rotation, maintaining only one pack in use at a time. A method of tamper-proof sealing of caps should be adopted to encourage good stock control, the presence of the seal being re-inforced by an appropriate label attached to every outer pack. It is also sensible to apply an in-use shelf-life to each pack so that the time after first opening is limited to a specific period. The success of such a procedure depends on the user recording the opening date clearly on the container label in a designated space.

## Table 1
## Code for Safe Storage and Use of Urine Testing Reagents

- Store at recommended temperature
- Apply an in-use shelf-life to each opened container
- Each outer container should have a tamper-proof seal which is broken when the bottle is opened for the first time
- Rotate stock, and have only one container in use at a time
- Replace caps tightly *immediately* after each opening
- Ensure the presence and patency of the desiccant
- Examine the feasibility of establishing a quality assurance programme for ward or clinic stocks.

**Quality Control and Quality Assurance**

Because reagent strips and tablets are relatively unstable if stored inappropriately, the need for routine quality control procedures to monitor strip performance from opened packs should be considered. Pharmacy departments include quality control staff with the expertise necessary to ensure the maintenance of the quality of medical products. Similar principles can be applied to items such as urine reagent tests. Because the correct performance of each and every strip is critical to clinical management of patients, reagent performance must be guaranteed throughout the in-use life of the pack. A pattern of regular checks on each in-use pack can be established, and the strips can be tested against suitable standards such as CHEK-STIX*.

*Regular quality control checks and staff training are important*

It should also be emphasised that staff training is an essential element of any quality assurance programme relating to urine testing materials. There are benefits to the patient, nurse, doctor and the hospital finances if an effective quality assurance programme is maintained which includes continuous product monitoring. It will ensure greater confidence in consistent test performance, fewer risks of errors, and less wastage.

*Quality assurance will benefit the patient, nurse, doctor and hospital finances*

An alternative approach to ensure performance for each strip or tablet would be to improve packaging systems. Clearly, individual hermetic sealing of each strip would effectively guarantee each strip at the point of use. However, such packaging does carry cost penalties.

## Table 2
### Elements of Quality Assurance of Urine Testing on Hospital Wards

| Responsibility | Role |
| --- | --- |
| Pharmacy | – Supply of tests<br>– Check stock rotation and levels<br>  Remove out-of-date material<br>– Check storage conditions<br>– Quality control of testing |
| Manufacturer | – Ward service<br>– Staff training<br>– Technical support |

### Conclusions

In conclusion, the purchase, storage and supply of urine reagent tablets and strips is a crucial aspect of safe testing at the bedside. Pharmacy staff are increasingly in demand at ward level to improve supply and stock control, and to improve clinical use of medicines through clinical pharmacy services.

Quality assurance of urine test reagents can form a part of this service.

# NOTES